"*The Fourth Moment: Journeys From the Known to the Unknown,* is in equal parts a woman's travel adventure and a mother's love letter to her children. With crisp prose and richly textured writing, Carole Garrison sheds light on Cambodia's dark history, and also its beautiful culture, sharing stories of what it means to be a mother, a daughter, and a family in our increasingly global world."

~ Loung Ung, author of *First They Killed My Father: A Daughter of Cambodia Remembers* (2006)

"*The Fourth Moment: Journeys From the Known to the Unknown* is a collection of memoir-essays, snapshots of life's big and small moments that lie just beyond the forgettable. These experiences bubble up unbidden into consciousness at the witching hour, or nudged into focus by something familiar, perhaps recorded in a locked diary, and if you're very lucky, shared with someone you love and trust. Garrison's stories are filled with sensory stimulation, colors, sounds, sights and aromas that sweeps across nations, through the sometimes tragic tales of friendships and romance, always infused with heartfelt warmth and longing. They lurk, then rear up demanding to be understood, processed and added to the body of knowledge that is both unique to you and part of the universal stream of life—fourth coming."

~Deborah DeNicola, author of *Future That Brought Her Here, The Memoir of a Call to Awaken* (2009)

"Garrison's stories are compelling. For example, 'Roaches' in Garrison's hands turns a base repugnancy into eloquent compassion. She somehow manages to weave a perfect description of their hardiness with today's political climate, and it all results in a resounding 'yeah!' in our minds at the end. This is a rare and true voice of an outsider looking in, and becoming comfortable, yet never forgetting that in our world, we are all, somehow, strangers in a strange land."

~Barbra Nightingale, poet, author and professor emeritus from Broward College, and Advisor Emeritus from Phi Theta Kappa

"Masterful! Garrison's extraordinary ability to take every day experiences and make them life learning treasures for the ages is almost ingenious. Walking the reader so generously through her failures and triumphs without pretense, with a lens of transparency she aims to redeem and transform the human spirit.

~Councilwoman Veronica Sims, Akron City, OH

"I know the author as 'Mamma.' She's been Mamma to us since moving to our small village in the summer of 1992, when I was eleven years old. Her stories are Cambodia's stories, and we lived them with her. Like her, these stories resonate with our challenges, passions and accomplishments. Be inspired."

~Sok, Keang, UNICEF, Phnom Penh, Cambodia

"Garrison cultivated her relations with Russian and Chinese members of the UN on a personal mission as an American to improve relations with them. She also was untiring in engaging with her many friends in the military from all countries to lobby for the acceptance of women fighters. It was a pleasure watching and learning from her can-do spirit."

~Kathleen Graff, International Red Cross (ICRC)

"As a political philosopher, I have long struggled with the question of how to live justly in a society comprised of people of different genders, races, religions, classes, ethnicities, and geographical locations. In her memoir, Carole J. Garrison provides the missing pieces to the puzzle. She makes the struggle for a just society personal. Whether it's growing up Jewish in 1950s America, or a 13-year-old girl's first encounter with racial segregation in the U.S. South, or a female police officer's orientation to the profession, Garrison articulates the effects of social disparities on the human heart with razor-like precision."

~Laura Newhart, professor of philosophy, Eastern Kentucky University

THE FOURTH MOMENT

THE FOURTH MOMENT
Journeys from the Known to the Unknown

A MEMOIR BY

CAROLE J. GARRISON

INTRODUCTION BY SARAH WILLIS

NEW YORK

www.2leafpress.org

P.O. Box 4378
Grand Central Station
New York, New York 10163-4378
editor@2leafpress.org
www.2leafpress.org

2LEAF PRESS
is an imprint of the
Intercultural Alliance of Artists & Scholars, Inc. (IAAS),
a NY-based nonprofit 501(c)(3) organization that promotes
multicultural literature and literacy.
www.theiaas.org

Book design and layout: Gabrielle David

Cover photo: Marilyn Howard, Copyright © 1991
Press Photo: Missica Skeens / Missica Photography, Copyright © 2017

Library of Congress Control Number: 2017932348

ISBN-13: 978-1-940939-63-6 (Paperback)
ISBN-13: 978-1-940939-64-3 (eBook)

10   9   8   7   6   5   4   3   2   1

Published in the United States of America

First Edition | First Printing

2LEAF PRESS trade distribution is handled by University of Chicago Press / Chicago Distribution Center (www.press.uchicago.edu) 773.702.7010. Titles are also available for corporate, premium, and special sales. Please direct inquiries to the UCP Sales Department, 773.702.7248.

To GG, my constant companion.

CONTENTS

INTRODUCTION 1

CAMBODIAN JOURNAL: PART ONE // 5

CHAPTER 1
Journal Entry: Through the Looking Glass 9

CHAPTER 2
Journal Entry: Giving up the Bones 13

CHAPTER 3
Journal Entry: A New Identity 19

CHAPTER 4
Journal Entry: Singing Contest 21

CHAPTER 5
Journal Entry: A Mother's Sacrifice 25

CHAPTER 6
Journal Entry: Lost in Translation 29

CHAPTER 7
Journal Entry: Clean Undies. 33

THE ROAD AHEAD // 37

CHAPTER 1
Evening in Paris. 41

CHAPTER 2
Sisters. 45

CHAPTER 3
Taboo. 49

CHAPTER 4
A Sliver of Ice Cream. 55

CHAPTER 5
Murder by Scripture. 57

CHAPTER 6
What Color is the Water?. 59

CHAPTER 7
A Scripted Life. 61

CHAPTER 8
Seeking Daddy 63

THE CONSTANT COMPANION // 67

CHAPTER 1
The Boarder 71

CHAPTER 2
Holding Mother's Hand. 75

CHAPTER 3
The Sewing Machine 79

CHAPTER 4
A Crosstown Bus 83

CHAPTER 5
The Little Red Suitcase 87

CHAPTER 6
Walking with Mom 91

BLIND SPOTS // 95

CHAPTER 1
Awakening to the Dream 99

CHAPTER 2
Bourgeoisie. 105

CHAPTER 3
No Choice is Free 109

CHAPTER 4
A Promise Made, a Promise Kept 113

CHAPTER 5
Rite of Passage 117

DETOURS // 121

CHAPTER 1
Bloody Palms 125

CHAPTER 2
Policewoman: Circa 1970s 127

CHAPTER 3
The VIP. 133

CHAPTER 4
Where's the Sugar?. 141

CAMBODIAN JOURNAL: PART TWO // 147

CHAPTER 1
Journal Entry: The Fire. 151

CHAPTER 2
Journal Entry: Angel of Buddha 165

CHAPTER 3
Journal Entry: Not Goodbye. 171

CHAPTER 4
Journal Entry: A Capital Offense 179

ROAD CLOSINGS AND U-TURNS // 191

CHAPTER 1
The Procedure. 195

CHAPTER 2
And the Truth Will Set You Free. 199

CHAPTER 3
Neighbors 203

CHAPTER 4
Sex Slaves. 205

CHAPTER 5
Busted 207

CHAPTER 6
Realizing A Slow Death 211

CHAPTER 7
The Bonus. 215

CHAPTER 8
Weaving Women's Colors 217

CHAPTER 9
A Seat At the Table 219

CHAPTER 10
The Last to Know. 223

CHAPTER 11
Synchronicity. 225

CHAPTER 12
DACOWITS and Regrets 227

CHAPTER 13
The Kindness of Strangers 231

CHAPTER 14
The Waiting Room. 233

LESSONS FROM ROADS LESS TRAVELED // 237

CHAPTER 1
Traveling Alone, Lonely Traveling 241

CHAPTER 2
She Must Be Crazy 245

CHAPTER 3
An Unfinished Rivalry. 249

CHAPTER 4
The Silent Scream 253

CHAPTER 5
An Intervention 257

CHAPTER 6
The Hajj 259

CHAPTER 7
Roaches 263

CAMBODIAN JOURNAL: PART THREE // 269

CHAPTER 1
Journal Entry: Kampongtrach Mountain 273

CHAPTER 2
Journal Entry: A Cambodian Pinocchio 277

CHAPTER 3
Journal Entry: Stolen 281

CHAPTER 4
Journal Entry: A Pilgrim's Journey 287

ABOUT THE AUTHOR. 293

OTHER BOOKS BY 2LEAF PRESS 297

INTRODUCTION

CAROLE GARRISON has always kept journals; notes to help her better understand the deeper meaning of her life and those she loves. She has been a daughter, a sister, a mother, a wife (and an ex-wife), a cop, a professor, an activist, a UN volunteer in Cambodia, a feminist, an observer and a participant, and much, much more. Here, in *The Fourth Movement,* Carole has culled and refined her collection of essays which explore, with humor and pathos, what it's like to be a woman in a vast, complicated world.

Over the years Carole's writing has taken me to so many fascinating places. Through her stories, I have learned what it was like to be a female cop in Atlanta in the 1970s. I have felt her struggle to find her voice and the inner strength to move forward amidst tremendous physical and metal challenges. I have learned about Cambodia and all the hard work it took to initiate their democratic election process. And through her stories I have met the people that she formed lasting friendships with, fascinating and diverse people of all nationalities and walks of life.

These stories in *The Fourth Movement* weave in and out of time, like pieces of a puzzle, building a larger picture of the whole — a life lived to its fullest. In this book, Carole touches on small telling moments, such as giving a young Cambodian girl a bottle of perfume, or simply riding a city bus and observing fellow passengers. She also writes to the momentous: a first visit to the Cambodian Killing Fields, the death of her father, even descriptions of sexual abuse. She takes us places we have never been, yet feel that we understand exactly what she has experienced, because she writes to the universal through the particular.

The opening chapters describe her year in Cambodia, when she volunteered with the UN to help organize Cambodia's first democratic election. But as Carole worked to change Cambodia's elections, Cambodia and its people helped to shape who Carole was to become: an activist and a mother of an adopted daughter from Cambodia.

Indeed, family and motherhood are a constant theme. At the center of this book is Carole's mother and her mother's failing health. We watch as Carole takes her mother to the doctors, or reads her father's love letters as her mother tells the story about how they met. Their relationship is sometimes thorny, sometimes sweet, and sometimes heartbreaking. I think we have all had this kind of relationship with someone we love. She takes us to all these emotional spaces we have ourselves occupied.

Carole is at heart a traveler who has seen amazing places and met amazing people, and she has the gift to write about what she has seen and felt. As she writes in the preface to one of the chapters: "I am most happy when I am wandering around, usually lost, in some foreign country where my travels reveal secrets not only about new and interesting places and people, but the ones that lead to new discoveries about myself."

By writing her memories, Carole tries to discover what is dishonest, and honest, and then where we go from there: our lessons learned.

But there is no beginning or ending to these stories. Each one is a nugget of its own, an "aha" moment, "those which stop you in your tracks, gut punch you, and force you to reconsider what you know and don't know. These moments are life's epiphanies when you become the student, rather than the teacher."

Stories like these are meant to be shared because they teach us that we each have our own questions, passions, insecurities and tribulations, and that we can prevail with our love intact if we keep our eyes open as well as our hearts. Along with an energy and passion to do everything she can for justice, she is open to connecting with humanity in every way possible. This is the stuff of these stories. I can't summarize them. You have to just read them, and see how they might connect with your own life; how they speak to you in particular about the bigger picture of being human.

Here's to the power of the written word to bring us all closer, to understand each other and the world beyond our own. ♦

— Sarah Willis, novelist and short story writer
The Sound of Us (Berkley 2005)

CAMBODIAN JOURNAL: PART ONE

Preface

Although I was passionate about going abroad, I despised uncertainty. I knew that my movie star handsome bartender boyfriend would not hang around waiting for me to return after his graduation from the University of Miami. A late bloomer to sex, I was absorbed in my first ever serious sexual relationship and was more randy than a dog in heat. Compounded with my insecurity, immaturity and self-doubt, I was in total despair over my fate. My choice was to catch a chronic disease in Afghanistan or convince my boyfriend to marry me so that I could live happily ever after and never worry about finding a job. Deciding on the latter option, I resigned my Peace Corps appointment.

Nearly thirty years later in 1992, I tried again to engage in international relations at the age of forty-nine. It might have been easier when I was twenty. ∎

CHAPTER 1

Journal Entry: Through the Looking Glass
UN Peacekeeping Mission
Phnom Penh, Cambodia 1992

S TEPPING OUT INTO THE NARROW DIRT LANE, I leaned my back against the cement block wall of the UN's guesthouse B in Phnom Penh, lit a cigarette and inhaled a puff of smoke along with the scents of sour fish soup, rice, and pork, greasy fried dough and savory noodles. I faced a bombed-out office-sized building, three stories high, with many of the walls missing or partially destroyed. The structure was home to at least one hundred people. They had no privacy. They lived inside and outside, in the yard and on the roof, eating, sleeping, playing cards, cooking over charcoal braziers and tending to dozens of children under the age of six. It had taken me a couple of days to figure out why all the children were so young: Cambodia had just emerged from two decades of death and more death. People were just starting to rebuild their lives, which were just like this wreckage of a building. Sometimes when the mothers

Typical Khmer woman living in the bombed out building across the road from the UN guesthouse B, 1992. *The Carole J. Garrison Family Archive.*

Carole being interviewed in her Women's Studies office for a news story before leaving for the UN's Cambodian peacekeeping mission, 1992. *The Carole J. Garrison Family Archive.*

saw me watching, they waved at me using their baby's hand. Other times, they ignored me.

But the sun—a fiery hot ball in the sky—was blinding, so I slipped beneath a sliver of shade from a wind-bent palm tree. I found myself looking directly into the face of a young woman. She wore a faded batik sarong skirt and a dirt-stained, white T-shirt. A pair of flimsy flip-flops was all that protected her feet from the thick layer of rubble and refuse that surrounded us. Her head was wrapped in a dusty red-and-white checkered *kramaa* that held her thick silky-black hair off her face, without keeping it under control. Her smooth bare café au lait skin glistened with sweat in the already too-hot morning sun. However, unlike many of the other girls her age, she was not pregnant—and no child held her hand.

There were only a few yards of the dirt-packed lane between us. Our eyes met and caught for the briefest of seconds, and then she looked down and nodded politely. Embarrassed to be caught staring, I did an awkward half-wave semi-bow thing while flicking my cigarette and crushing it into the dirt. Unable to speak, having no language training beyond my fifteen important and must-know Khmae phrases for tourists in Cambodia, I was alarmed when she walked toward me. Still, I felt utterly compelled to grab the moment, to connect to this life and to begin living it. Hoping to communicate with her through hand gestures, I set my coffee cup down and returned my lighter to my pocket.

The lighter clinked against a small vial of perfume I had brought from the States. The girl continued to approach, and impetuously I shoved the tiny bottle into her hand. She was confused. So was I. Yet I couldn't just walk away. Taking the perfume back, I dabbed it on her neck, then mine. As if playing charades, I inhaled the perfume, closed my eyes and tried to convey my best impression of bliss.

Her dark eyes grew wide as I gave her back the vial. She

put the bottle to her nose and sniffed. Her nose wrinkled, and then grinning, she dabbed the perfume on her neck. I nodded my approval, but then she put some on her hair and teeth and poured the rest on her clothes. I was helpless to intervene. And what could I say, even if I spoke her language? Could I tell her that she was going to smell like an escapee from a cheap whorehouse? Her family would probably make her sleep out in the street for a week.

I was in some Asian version of *Through the Looking Glass* where things looked familiar but were anything but. This was the place I chose to find salvation from my stale life at home? This was where I hoped to become a hero? Maybe, I thought, I'd better start rethinking my plan.♦

CHAPTER 2

Journal Entry: Giving up the Bones
UN Peacekeeping Mission
Phnom Penh, Cambodia 1992

COME ON, COME," the teachers shouted and waved to us as my roommate Beatrice and I ambled lazily into the classroom. Mr. Tong, director of the United Nations' cultural training for its volunteers in Cambodia, was looking quite out of character as he checked his wristwatch and tapped his foot on the scarred, stained tile floor.

"We are going in the vans to the national Killing Fields monument this morning. The drive will take about forty-five minutes to an hour," he informed us in his formal, quiet voice. Like others in the room, I made an involuntary sucking sound. We had all read about the Killing Fields. They dotted the landscape across the country, but few were marked. Most were located on mountainsides, their horror reclaimed by the jungle. But the terror was palpable in the ruins of Phnom Penh and in the stories of the locals, who gave muted explanations of missing parents or siblings.

I thought about Hun, the young, multilingual money changer I'd befriended, who had hidden in the jungle at night to escape Pol Pot's guards. After her relatives were murdered in their bed for speaking French, and her parents arrested, Khmer Rouge soldiers had sent her to a children's work camp, saying, "Intellectuals don't make good rice farmers." She had showed me her missing toe—a punishment for disobedience. As a middle-aged American in the 1990s, I had no personal experience with that kind of pain or fear—except for what I'd imagined from reading books, seeing movies and hearing the stories of the few family members who had survived the Holocaust or the Russian pogroms.

Turning my attention to the van, I took a seat by the window, hoping to open it and catch a breeze. As I struggled to open the window, we drove past the Royal Palace and turned down an unfamiliar, narrow alleyway. Beatrice, sitting in the row ahead, pointed out the sign above a sleazy bar around the corner from the palace: "Welcome to the Heart of Darkness." I reached over the seat and put a clammy hand on her shoulder. It seemed ominously prescient of our destination.

We continued out of the city on a dirt road lined with makeshift stands selling fruit, cigarettes and bottles of petrol for motorbikes. A thick layer of red parched dirt covered everything, cloaking the countryside in what looked like a film of blood. Coughing, I pulled the window closed.

About fifteen kilometers outside of Phnom Penh in the village of Choeung Ek, we arrived at the monument to the infamous Killing Fields of Pol Pot, which memorialized the genocide that had claimed nearly three million victims—one-third of the country's population. As the vans of UN volunteers pulled into a parking area, I could see only a chalky white field with a tall pagoda in the center. We tumbled out of the cramped vans, hot from the dusty ride, and collected rather haphazardly around the stone entrance. A slim young Cambodian man named Kosal greeted us. Putting our hands together, as if we were going to pray, we chanted in unison, "Sue-saw-day Kosal," wishing him good day.

Kosal began his standard orientation to the site in heavily accented but reasonably good English. "Cambodians," he said stiffly, "do not liken this genocide to Hitler's."

Cambodians claimed the slaughter to be more terrible, because it was brother killing brother. The tortuous ways that people were killed, often by having their heads bashed in or suffocated with plastic grocery bags and drowned, were equally as terrible. Despite Kosal's denial of a Holocaust comparison, images of skeletal figures piled fourteen deep in a forty-foot-long ditch flashed before me. My eyes squinted in the bright sun as I stood immobilized and stared.

I moved closer to the *stupah*, the monument erected in memory of the victims. It was not a Western museum paying homage to the dead. Glass cabinets held neither grainy photos of those who had died nor yellowed pages of recovered diaries. The mementos were the dead themselves, who had been excavated from the hundreds of mass graves that surrounded the area. Behind clear exterior glass windows, shelves upon shelves of skulls—many with large holes from being bludgeoned—lay in silent testimony. Mothers, daughters, fathers and sons had been buried unceremoniously en masse, then exhumed and displayed—unmarked, unidentifiable and unclaimed. The Killing Fields were a never-ending national funeral that did little to celebrate life. Instead, the skulls told the story of incomprehensible death.

Kosal, who had lost many relatives, took us to some of the excavated sites. As I walked, something crunched beneath my feet. I looked more closely. I found teeth and bits of bone everywhere. My stomach turned over as the quiet chalky earth gave up its secret. A sort of fear struck me and prickled my skin as I walked. This horror touched me as I touched it. I walked in the graves; I walked among the dead.

Pagoda of skulls, Killing Fields Memorial in Phnom Penh, Cambodia (1992). *The Carole J. Garrison Family Archive.*

When the tour was over, I took Kosal's hand and said, "Good-bye. This was too terrible. I won't forget what happened here."

From my seat in the van on our way back to the city, I saw plastic bags fluttering from tree limbs and bushes, reminding me of their past use as instruments of suffocation. With every patch of white gravel we passed, I imagined a pile of human bones crushed and forgotten.

Suddenly Hun's face appeared. It was an apparition, but I saw her—small and frightened, running from the Khmer Rouge soldiers with plastic bags and machetes in their hands. Then she disappeared—maybe hidden and safe? No, the soldiers were dragging her back to the work camp and cutting off her toe as punishment. There was blood, but no tears.

My breath stuck in my lungs, and my chest tightened with a new appreciation of Hun's unspeakable experience. I was suffering with her. Earlier pity gave way to compassion and understanding. By comparison, what had happened to me? I had run away from an enviable career—albeit stale and safe—as well as a passionless but financially comfortable relationship, to have an adventure organizing Cambodia's first democratic election. Hun and I didn't inhabit the same universe.

Back in class, we followed up our outing with a lesson in cultural differences. I mentioned my generous tip to the guide and my response to Kosal's obvious pain. Mr. Tong looked at me and chuckled loudly. "Ms. Garrison, this guide, this young man you met at the Killing Fields, knows exactly how to generate a large tip!"

My face flushed red and my fists clenched. I tried to keep my voice even and steady. "I wonder exactly what you consider the appropriate tip for a man who guides you by his family's skulls as you crush the remains of their bones with each step." There was no sound in the classroom; not even the fans moved. Mr. Tong met my glare, but he only smiled politely and nodded his head.♦

CHAPTER 3

Journal Entry: A New Identity
UN Peacekeeping Mission
Phnom, Penh, Cambodia 1992

WOVEN REED MATS COVERED THE FLOOR. There were no chairs in this dingy white washed room and nothing resembling a dining suite. I sat down alongside Beatrice, as instructed, and the two old women handed out plates and spoons. Savanreit put the bowls of bysal and meat in front of us. "Pork, beef and rice, eat please," she said reassuringly, taking her place on the mat beside us. "They cooked all morning for you."

Savanreit, our French-Khmer language teacher, had invited my French roommate Beatrice and me to lunch a few weeks after we had arrived in Cambodia to join the United Nation's peacekeeping mission, UNTAC.

The elderly women sat cross-legged on floor mats, chewing on areca nuts wrapped in betel leaf—a mild sedative, popular in Southeast Asia for centuries. Smiling at us through reddish-brown stained teeth, they talked to us in Khmae, as if we understood everything they said.

Savanreit noticed me staring at her mother and her aunt's teeth. "The elderly spent long days harvesting rice under the Khmer Rouge. My mother and her sister were city raised, not on the *ferme*, ah pardon, the farm. The soldiers cruelly beat them to work faster. Now they chew the leaf to calm themselves, to forget," she told me nonchalantly. I felt a knot of shock in my stomach.

Following lunch, I stayed seated on the woven reed mats and politely watched a video of Cambodian fashions and dance on a small nineteen-inch TV. Bent over from beatings in Pol Pot's labor camp, one of the old women sat next to me, gently patting my hand and smiling up at me with her stain-toothed grin.

The touch of her warm, brown gnarled hands soothed me. Reluctantly, I pulled my hands away and unfastened my coral beaded necklace. "Here Auntie, this is for you," I said, hoping that she understood my impetuous gift. She beamed her betel-leaf smile, and Savanreit translated. "My auntie is happy today; it is the first time she meets Untac's people and someone from Untac gives her a present." I was now officially Untac — not professor, not ex-wife, not mother or any of my prior identities. ◆

CHAPTER 4

Journal Entry: Singing Contest

UN Peacekeeping Mission
Village of Skon, Kâmpóng Cham Provence, Cambodia, 1992

I HAD BEEN ASSIGNED TO ORGANIZE the election in the district of Cheong Prey, and had found a traditional—no plumbing or wiring—house in Skon, the district's main market town. I had negotiated a deal with the Chinese officers of the engineering battalion billeted there to run electricity from their institutional generator to my little abode.

"It's too friggin' hot. I'm not lifting one more box or moving one more piece of furniture until we get a friggin' fan," I wailed.

No one responded because no one else was there. My roommate wouldn't arrive for a few more days, not until the house was wired and the fans working. I swiped at my face with a T-shirt already wet from sweat and red from the roadside dust that poured in through the glassless windows from outside.

I rode my bike over to the Chinese engineering battalion so I could give the barracks commander more U.S. silver dollars in order to keep diplomatic relations on an even keel and to start the electricity from their generator flowing to my house on

Carole and Captain Yuan, my back channel to electric power, at the Chinese military barracks, Skon, Kâmpóng Cham, Cambodia 1992, the location of the singing contest. *The Carole J. Garrison Family Archive.*

the far side of the village's central market. As it turned out, we hadn't bought enough red wire, so I marched off to the market, the major's English-speaking captain in tow. We found a small stall in the market that made do as a makeshift electoral supply store—walked to the house I would soon occupy—back to the Chinese barracks—to return once again to the house. I think these guys may have known something about building roads and bridges, but not much about electrical wiring.

When I returned to the village the next day, the bright red wire from the Chinese battalion to my house was up and connected. Click. The fans worked, the small desk light next to my bed worked. The refrigerator didn't. I biked over to the barracks to thank the captain and sergeant, and more importantly, to see if they could up the amps so I could get the refrigerator to cool.

Inside the big chain link fence that protected the camp and grounds, I could see groups of thirty men, each parading around the field in parade right order, but given they were engineering corps not combat infantry, the display lacked the military precision one expects from marching soldiers. Instead of a rifle, each soldier carried a small chair with him. In stiff formation, they arrived as a unit in front of a five-chair reviewing stand, opened their little chairs and sat down.

I stood next to my bike, unconcerned about the afternoon sun beating down on my unprotected head, my face pressed against the fencing. I began to wonder if I stumbled across a Chinese rendition of the movie *Stripes*. The similarities continued as one member of the group, standing rigid and red-faced gave a little speech to the officers on the dais. Soldiers and chairs would shift around a little more and then the group would sing.

I once heard music like that before, in an alley around the corner from the Forbidden City in Beijing—a Chinese opera. To my untrained ear, it sounded like cats brawling while out on their late night prowl.

The songs were in Chinese, the tunes unfamiliar. Cats are more musical—no *American Idol* winners there. Still, I wanted to applaud, I wanted to cheer and yell out bravo, bravo—but I stayed quiet, I didn't want to intrude. The universe had gifted me with a singular event. I was grateful and wanted to share my good fortune. Too bad this is one of those stories where "you had to be there."♦

CHAPTER 5

Journal Entry: A Mother's Sacrifice
UN Peacekeeping Mission
Skon, Kâmpóng Cham, Cambodia 1992

STILL AIR, HEAVY WITH THE SCENT of jasmine and bamboo, filled the empty house. Indeed, even my cat, Fannett, was out prowling the dirt alleyways of Skon. I liked the quiet, but I liked it just as well when the house was full of the giggles, tinkling laughter and shy looks exchanged among the three little neighbor girls who reminded me that Cambodia was worth saving. *They also reminded me how much of my daughters' childhood I had missed.*

As I was wondering where they were, I heard a soft knocking at my door. I opened it to see Moam-Moam with a woman I had not met before. The girl, already soft and round at eleven, was a coffee-colored Cambodian beauty. She tossed her long, curly hair and smiled with her straight, small white teeth sparkling in contrast to her dark skin. Then she looked down at the floor.

"Momma," Moam-Moam said, *"Kynome madai."*

Moam-Moam's mother, in her mid to late forties, was

dark-skinned and small; she was shabbily dressed in a dirty cotton sarong and sleeveless blouse. She was of classic Cambodian ethnicity, with no hint of Chinese blood in her features. Beaten down by poverty and life, she smiled, showing a gold tooth cap that glittered in her mouth. Without forewarning, she said, "Moam-Moam make you happy in America. She is good girl and like you much." No hinting, no coyness. She wanted me to take Moam-Moam to the U.S. with me, raise her as my daughter and make her a "gold bar child." That's what the locals called the lucky ones who escaped Cambodia's unrelenting poverty.

"No more school for Moam-Moam, *klai nah* (too expensive)," the woman said as if she needed to add a final justification.

A heavy silence descended, almost squeezing the air out of the room. I stood thinking. She stared down at her bare feet.

By that time, I wasn't shocked by my naivety, as I had been in my earlier encounter with my Cambodian language teacher—who had taken me by surprise when she asked me to adopt her small daughter and take her to the U.S. I had now been in Cambodia long enough to know that these women were not choosing to give up their daughters. No, I thought, they were driven by poverty and the hope that their sacrifice would lead to a better life for their children. There was no shame in their requests, just hope born of desperation.

I liked Moam-Moam. In fact, she represented everything that was innocent and beautiful about Cambodia. I had no grandchildren, many resources at home and a life without a partner. I struggled with my affection for Moam and the idea of adopting her. No, I had boundaries, and I had hardened myself to the reality of Cambodians' insatiable neediness. I couldn't take on this fight. It was all that I could do to survive.

"Moam-Moam *saa-at,* beautiful," I told her mother. In expectation, the woman raised her eyes to meet mine. "Nevertheless," I said, shaking my head to indicate no. "I cannot take her to the U.S.," I noted, with some disappointment, a flicker of relief

Moam-Moam and her mother after I told them that I could not adopt Moam-Moam and take her back to America, in Skon, Kâmpóng Cham, Cambodia, 1992 *The Carole J. Garrison Family Archive.*

crossing Moam-Moam's face. Her mother's face betrayed nothing. She put her hands together in a formal thank you gesture, bowed and left the house, with Moam-Moam following in her wake. I stood in the door way watching them walk across the road to the small wooden shack where they lived. Moam-Moam turned and glanced once in my direction, her expression unreadable, then hurried to catch up with her mother. I let out a deep sigh, but not of relief. Instead, I felt a pang of regret creeping deep down into the pit of my stomach.

Sitting on a chair as dusky shadows darkened the room, I imagined Moam-Moam in my house in Akron—her face flush with excitement over her new life and her smile lighting up the air around us, as she and I hugged and laughed together. In this vision, she was safely away from the absolute poverty that was her destiny in Skon.♦

CHAPTER 6

Journal Entry: Lost in Translation

UN Peacekeeping Mission
Skon, Kâmpóng Cham, Cambodia 1992

"For countless reasons, there will be no voting machines in Cambodia; voters will simply mark their ballot with an X, according to the UN election protocol." My housemate and I looked at each other with dismay and consternation as our electoral supervisor gave this report. We knew better. The Cambodian people couldn't wrap their minds around using an age-old symbol for danger to indicate their preferred leader. It was simply an anathema to them.

I SAW OUR HOUSEKEEPER through the screen door. She stood, arms folded tightly across her chest, a scowl frozen on her normally relaxed and smiling face. I looked from her to my French housemate, Bea, who had just emerged from her bedroom, and raised my eyebrows in question. "What the hell?"

"Em, I don't know, *ma chérie.* You must ask her."

Of course I couldn't ask; I couldn't speak her language. I pushed open the door and gestured for the woman to enter our house. She stood resolutely. She wasn't moving. Bea brushed past me, and we stood together in the doorway, unsure what to do. Using my limited knowledge of Khmae, I pleaded, *"Som toh, lukswray, Neang."* She was stone.

Then Bea tried in French. *"Qu'y a-t-il?" "Quel est le problème?"* Neang's blank stare suggested she was not among those Khmer who still spoke French, a vestige of France's occupation of Cambodia during the colonial period.

I was about to give up, shut the door, and empty my own red plastic chamber pot when Neang's arm flew up and pointed to the door. I peered around to the front of it and saw the sign that Bea and I had put up as a joke.

The red square sign was ubiquitous in post-war, ravaged Cambodia. The image of the skull and crossbones, an X, spoke in every language — stop, keep out, danger — while the printed English words said, "Danger, land mines." We had used a liquid correction pen to blot-out 'land mines' and insert the word "women," a joke our housekeeper obviously didn't get.

I grabbed the sign and pulled it off the door. *"Aut panyaha,* no problem," I continued to plead, pointing at the large white X. Her eyes wide open, Neang cautiously poked her head into the room. I assume to look about for some sign of land mines or other dangers. *"Aut panyaha,"* I repeated. Bea pointed to the word "women" and said, *"Neang, aut boom-boom."* In desperation, I summoned my interpreter, who explained our jest to the wary housekeeper.

Neang nodded, the scowl still on her face — a rebuke of our ignorant behavior — then walked past Bea and me into the house and began her chores.

Bea and I protested. "How could the UN expect Cambodians to use an X to designate their choice for a leader? How could the UN miss the cultural significance of something so embedded in the country's psyche?" We wondered out loud if the guys like our supervisor, who ran the electoral unit, had ever talked to a Cambodian or even to anyone who had met a Cambodian, prior to writing the protocol.

Of course, we only knew the answers to our questions because we had already seen the response to our own cultural incompetence a few days before the briefing.♦

CHAPTER 7

Journal Entry: Clean Undies

UN Peacekeeping Mission
Pouthisat Town, Pouthisat, Cambodia 1993

VEATA, MY CAMBODIAN HOUSEKEEPER, presented me with a favorite meal—eggplant and pork, rice and sautéed veggies. It was not quite twilight, and the banana leaves outside my window looked more gray than green in the rapidly dimming light. I was enjoying my meal when I heard two loud explosions like distant thunder. My walkie-talkie—my constant companion—crackled, and an urgent voice demanded my immediate attention. "Mine explosions, near the soccer field where the Royalist political party is to hold its rally in the morning."

As the world around me darkened, I slid under my mosquito net for the night. The radio, silent again, lay beside my pillow. I heard several more loud booms. The air in my room vibrated and the noise filled my ears. This time the booms were big-gun volleys from somewhere not too distant. I waited, holding my breath for more explosions. I remembered that gun lobs were like lightning; if you could hear them, the rockets weren't hitting you.

The radio crackled alive again. "Several casualties, mostly workers preparing for the rally at the soccer field. Khmer Rouge guerillas have engaged the KPAF with fire from several directions." The bulletin ended with a warning to turn off all lights and take immediate shelter. Shelter? Where?

There was no place to hide. I slunk out of bed and slipped into some clothes, in case I had to leave quickly. I could hardly see in the darkness. Slowly I made my way to the door and walked down the steps leading to the bottom half of the house. I wanted to calm my housekeeper and her relatives, who had fled the outlying villages, as well as some staff who were also staying there that night. Almost everyone was outside, milling around in the courtyard of the tiny compound.

"*Soom toh,* put out any candles, and *aut pluen,* no lights," I said. "Mr. Om, tell them to go inside and keep everything dark so we are not a target for rockets. *Aut panyaha,* we are okay. Go inside," I repeated.

"Momma, come stay with us," Mr. Om pleaded, as if reading my mind. "Wooden house not good if rocket hits."

The vein under my eye pulsed, and my upper lip began to twitch. It would be easy to infect the others with my fear and panic, so I climbed back upstairs, knowing they were safer in the stone part of the house. So why was I going upstairs?

Unbidden, my mother's classic advice spilled into consciousness: "Always be sure to wear clean underwear, in case you are in an accident." I was lying back in bed with my T-shirt and clean undies on, silencing my mother's voice, when I felt a rumble followed by a flash that lit up the sky white-yellow. The house shook; then the boom of big guns rippled across my body, and my ears started ringing. Someone was banging on the door and shouting, "Momma, Momma." It was Mr. Om, the staff driver.

Thinking we were under attack, everyone downstairs ran back outside again when the blast swept over them, rattling walls and windows and dishes. The dogs were spooked and barking, but the radio was silent. As I stood at the top of the stairs, the fear rising from the people below was palpable. Terror had frozen us all in place.

Once again, the radio crackled back to life. "This is Poppa 2. The guns firing now are pointing away from the town. The immediate threat has passed. All medical personnel should report to HQ immediately. Collateral casualties, please report immediately on channel 9. Everyone else should remain in place."

"*Aut panyaha,*" I said weakly to Mr. Om. "Tell everyone to go back inside. We are safe." Not believing myself, I crept back to my bed. I felt as if I had been on a roller coaster ride, coming down the last hill before making a hairpin turn into the dock. The ride slowed as it entered the exit gate and stopped. I fell into an uneasy sleep.◆

THE ROAD AHEAD

Preface

Most childhood memories fade, pruned along with weak or unused neural connections. Psychologists call this inability childhood or infantile amnesia. A few memories survive this pruning, usually the very emotional ones. And some that are apparently lost have actually remained with us — albeit in a different form. The ones that linger into adulthood are those that, for good or ill, haunt our dreams and shape our lives. ■

CHAPTER 1

Evening in Paris

I WAS SURE ANYONE WITHIN ten feet of me could hear my heart pounding. It was beating wildly like a staccato drum from deepest Africa. I only guessed that, since my only experience with Africa had been the black-and-white *Tarzan* movie I saw a couple of months back at the Saturday matinee. Still, what I felt was nothing like I had ever experienced in my nine years of living.

THE AISLE AT THE BIG WOOLWORTH'S five-and-dime store was empty, except for me. I was looking at the row of tiny, three-inch-tall cobalt blue bottles that were labeled in silver script, "Evening in Paris." Smelling its powdery, seductive floral aroma in the tester, I was sure my mother would think it was divine. Mother's Day was the following Sunday, and I had no gift for her yet. A bottle cost $1.20 plus a penny tax—a fortune, and a dollar more than I had in my tiny change purse.

I picked up one of the small glass vials, turning it this way and that, shaking it gently to make sure it was full of liquid, and then clutched it so tightly that it began to feel warm. Its contents were hardly visible when I closed my fingers around it. My pulse quickened. The pocket of the apron my mother made me wear over my dress to keep it clean was roomy and deep. My heart raced as I dropped the small vial into it and walked out through the heavy glass door to the sidewalk.

I walked down the street as nonchalantly as I was could, all the while listening for shouts or footsteps behind me. A shop door banging, a person rushing past, and the backfire of a car all sent me reeling with fright. Nevertheless, high on a rush of adrenalin, I let out a shout of pure exhilaration when I could finally see the grey shingled house on Pratt Avenue in the distance. I had escaped undetected, and I got my mother's present. She would be so happy with her perfume, so happy with me.

"Happy Mother's Day," I said, thrusting the small package over the kitchen table and into her hand. My mother threw me a sideways glance as she pulled the bottle from the tissue paper, dramatically unscrewed the tiny cap, and inhaled the scent. I waited breathlessly for her reaction, for her to enfold me in her arms. But her smile was tight. Disappointed, I was afraid she didn't care for the smell. Her eyebrows knitted together as she turned the small bottle in her hand, looking from it to me. Instead of embracing me as I expected, she only mumbled, "Thank you."

She knew! She would tell my father I was a thief. She would regret that I was her daughter. My adrenalin high slipped inexorably into a swamp of misery and shame. I waited sullenly for the other shoe to drop.

It never did. My mother's strategy was simply to let me know that she knew. My self-inflicted chastisement that came with the anticipation of reprisal far exceeded any punishment she could meet out herself.

I have since taken the occasional stapler home from work or pocketed a pen from the bank—each time reliving the shame from my childhood heist. More often, I point out to a cashier that

I was undercharged on my purchase, or I run back to pay for an item that went unnoticed in the back corner of my shopping cart—each action a form of penance for my earlier misdeed.

Iconic bottles of this chic French perfume can still be found in junk stores across the United States and on e-bay, coveted by women with memories of World War II romances wrapped in its scent. And I've heard that Macy's is now selling the fragrance, which has recently been reissued. But for me, the cobalt blue color of its bottle will always be an antidote to taking what does not belong to me.♦

CHAPTER 2

Sisters

MY PARENTS HAD NAMED ME Joy, Carole Joy. Daddy said it was because I, his only daughter, was his joy. But when I was almost five, they brought her home. Why? We had been the textbook family, two boys and a girl, each the perfect two-and-a-half years apart. Although I didn't know it then, my dad would pass away before I turned twelve. But he was already sick, and I reasoned another baby wasn't good for his health; certainly, I was enough. I was his joy.

She became his sunshine. They even named her Sunnie. I detested her.

When she was about three years old, I formed a plan. Late at night, I would sneak out of bed and warily creep to the bathroom, listening for any indication that my parents or brothers might be awake and catch me. My heart pounding with anticipation, I would fill a plastic cup with water, warm water, and carry it in both hands—making sure not to spill a single drop until I stood over her bed. Then slowly, so as not to wake her,

Carole, 1945 Still daddy's special girl (and only daughter). *The Carole J. Garrison Family Archive.*

Typical childhood studio photograph back in the day with my siblings: (from left) David, Nat, Carole and Sunnie. Chicago, IL, 1949. In those early days we were a happy bunch of kids. *The Carole J. Garrison Family Archive.*

I would let the water dribble down over her PJs until they were soaking wet.

"I don't understand. I don't even let her have a drink before bedtime, even though she begs me. Why is she still wetting the bed?" Daddy would say as he hugged her, shook his head sadly and mutter something about her growing out of it. I would watch from the hallway feeling smug while trying to conceal my glee over what I hoped was her reduced status in his affection.

On my fortieth birthday, I finally confessed my childish sin to my mother. I probably shouldn't have. She became a typhoon of swirling anger.

I refer to my sister as Sunnie now. I guess my parents were right all along.♦

CHAPTER 3

Taboo

I LOOKED AT THE WHITE BUSINESS ENVELOPE and sighed—probably another page of mailing labels from a needy cause requesting a donation. In the Trump era, I figured that every organization had its hand out for good reason, but I already had a zillion mailing labels and was pretty full up on my charitable donations: West Virginia Public Broadcasting, VFW, St. Jude's, the Smithsonian and The Nature Conservancy, among others. I was about to pitch the envelope into the recycling pile when I noticed it was from the Center for Disease Control. Hmm, I thought. The CDC doesn't ask for donations...at least not yet.

The enclosed letter explained that the center was offering a forty-dollar gift to volunteers willing to take the 2017 National Injury and Health Survey. What the heck! I called the number and a sweet-voiced girl answered.

After several minutes of caveats, disclaimers and instructions, we began the survey. It took me far less time to realize that it wasn't about falls and injuries, a fear of mine as I approach old age; rather, it was primarily about sexual violence between intimate partners. Although I had little personal experience with this worthy topic, as a Criminal Justice and Women's Studies professor I knew all about the problem of domestic violence. The survey did touch briefly, however, on my own experience with childhood sexual abuse.

Just answering the questions released a flood of raw emotions and a rekindling of the intense anger that I'd carried around in my wounded child psyche for close to four decades. I glanced at the little card that I'd stuck in a photo stand by my desk as a reminder: I can release the past and forgive everyone. Nope, guess I can't. At that moment my anger and sadness were equivalent to my MMPI scores when I was ending a very long relationship.

Back then, in 1991, when my shrink's business partner scored my psychology profile, he told her that he hoped he never had to meet me.

"Why?" Ingrid asked.

"Are you kidding? I've never seen anger scores in this range; she's over the top," he replied.

"She's a feminist, and she's going through a breakup," Ingrid offered by way of an explanation.

"Nope, sorry. That doesn't account for scores this high. Glad she's your client and not mine," he countered and wished her "good luck."

Knowing I would need her support to get through the ordeal and continue to handle my job demands, I had employed Ingrid—a nice-looking woman in her early forties—as my therapist. We worked through my relationship angst and probed into the other loose ends of my adult life. Issues with children, an earlier marriage, careers and lovers were all reviewed until, finally, Ingrid said we needed to work on my wounded child within. Although I was not happy then, I was functional. I got up every morning, dressed, worked, ate—albeit mostly Cream of Wheat. I figured I was doing fine!

"Carole, I really think that all of this—all the unlearned, repetitive mistakes—stem from your early sexual abuse," Ingrid said as she tried to cajole me into discussing it. But I resisted, as I had resisted for nearly forty years.

I know that the sodomy began in the 1940s, shortly after I turned seven, and lasted till I was almost nine. But repressed memories have a way of burrowing so deeply into the recesses of the mind that they cannot be recaptured, even for a writer's needs. Something shocking happens, and the mind pushes the events into some inaccessible corner of the subconscious.

So as the years went on, I forgot the details. I only remembered—remembered vividly—the emotions: shame, guilt, fear. We didn't talk about sex in my family. At first, I was uncertain whether his touching me and asking me to touch his genitals was wrong. I knew him. No one had told me not to trust him. In fact, no one had warned me about big people in general and, at seventeen, he was a big person to me. His threats brought the notion that this is a bad thing. I don't remember his actual warnings about what would happen if I spoke about our secret, but I do remember that they scared me.

This bad thing was rewarded by gifts for my silence in the form of fashion dolls, like today's Barbies, but dressed in different costumes from countries around the world. No one had noticed my growing collection of dolls—my dad was seriously ill and my mother was distracted.

Eventually I told them. I don't remember the details of my confession, as they are lost in the same dusty back bin of my mind as his precise actions and warnings. I was not privy to how my parents dealt with my teenage offender, but he was gone from my life and the family resumed a sense of normalcy as if nothing had occurred.

I didn't go back to normal, however. I had a new normal. My parents remained silent, so I couldn't express my anxieties to them. Not knowing if my violator had been punished, I could only assume that I was at fault.

At the age of ten, I would take long walks and practice saying swear words, sometimes shouting them out loud like a person with Tourette Syndrome. I liked how they sounded; I liked that they were forbidden, that they made me feel powerful. Later, I was labeled a prude by the boys in high school—an iron maiden. I was not sexually active in college, either; eventually I pursued and married the first boy-man with whom I had a physical relationship. My frigidity and guilt about anything sexual was a problem, but not nearly the problem of my rage.

Not long after my therapy sessions with Ingrid ended, my mother came to visit to console me and help me settle into my newly single life. I had rejected more therapy but turned my unresolved anger on her. "Why didn't you protect me, help me to heal?" I demanded.

There were no excuses, hugs or teary eyes. She didn't mention my father's illness or my siblings' needs. As best as I can recall, there was a tinge of sadness in her voice but nothing more to reveal any emotion when she replied, "My father's best friend sexually abused me when I was a girl; I survived, so I figured you would too."

So that was it. She couldn't help me because no one had helped her. I was not about to harass a septuagenarian who had done the best she could. I was finished being angry with her. I forgave her. I absolved my abuser. I excused my family. I forgave myself. I begged the universe to do the same and the rage disappeared. Hate had eaten me up for decades. I was sure that compassion, love and forgiveness had cured me...until I took the survey.

The renewed pain lasted for only a few hours after completing the research study—though long enough to motivate me to write the CDC, critique its survey and suggest that it be reconfigured so that older subjects have the opportunity to share the horrific impact of childhood sexual abuse on a person's life. Because this form of abuse is still a taboo topic in our society, the survey served to remind me that children, who were sodomized like I was, are still struggling in silence.

I did survive and eventually thrived. Will they?◆

CHAPTER 4

A Sliver of Ice Cream

MY FIRST MEMORABLE EXPERIENCE with unfair treatment came when I was eight. Embarrassment crawled up my neck and into my cheeks, reddening my skin. Outrage mixed with disbelief as my mother, my protector, holding the tray of home-made ice cream, lifted her arm and pointed with her extended index finger, commanding me to go to my room. I continued to protest. "It wasn't me, I promise I did not eat the ice cream." My mother was unrelenting.

"Look here young lady, do you see this? Someone has taken a slice of ice cream from the tray. Your brothers told me it was you. You're tall enough to reach the freezer. You've had your desert, now go to your room."

My protests turned to sobs. "I didn't, I didn't." But my tears and sniffles fell on deaf ears, just as my protests had. I climbed the stairs to my bedroom. I had been shamed, unfairly punished. I had been framed!

Weeks later my mother made her, infamous by my calculations, ice cream again. Dinner was over and my eldest brother rushed over to the freezer to retrieve the tin ice cube tray of frozen confectionary. He held it in his hand and bawled, "Mom, she did it again." Mother ran over and looked at the tray. My dad joined her.

"I don't know," she said patting her lips and carefully examining the missing slice of ice cream. "It's the same size and shape as last time. Oh dear, I think the mix just shrinks when it cools."

I was absolved, found innocent of the crime. I wanted remorse from my mother, I wanted her contrition. I asked for a double helping and an apology. I got neither. It was the most unfair of all.

"Carole, think of all the times you have done something that I didn't catch. Just consider your punishment for all those things you've gotten away with."

I wonder if these lessons in fairness develop in everyone as we matured into the understanding of real unfairness or injustice, like poverty, genocide, starvation, natural disasters—often the result of nothing more than one's skin tone, religion, or accident of birth or geography. I came to understand the meaning of "But not for the grace of God go I."♦

CHAPTER 5

Murder by Scripture

I GREW UP IN THE ONLY single-family house within a square block on the near-north side of Chicago. The neighborhood was predominantly Catholic and Jewish. My best friends, four of the eight King kids, lived next door in one of the gray stones that lined most of the street.

"We can't play with you," Mary said one day, standing awkwardly at the front door as I approached her house.

"Why not?" I replied.

"You killed Christ—we don't play with murderers."

Intolerance starts young, before we are old enough to recognize it and put up our defenses.♦

CHAPTER 6

What Color is the Water?

W E MOVED FROM CHICAGO'S FRIGID winters to Florida's balmy weather in the early 1950s, a futile attempt to extend my father's tenuous hold on life. Our house—a typical square, pastel- painted, cement-block, slab-construction dwelling—was on the wrong side of the Tamiami Trail but close to the upscale city of Coral Gables. At thirteen, I could catch a bus from our corner to the terminal near the theater in the center of town.

Open and airy, the bus station was comprised of a series of large paddocks, a small building housing public toilets, some well-groomed tropical plants and two drinking fountains—unnoticed by me until one steamy August afternoon. I bounced off the bus, my change purse clutched in my hand, and set off to meet my girlfriends for a matinee showing of *Love Me Tender*. Spotting the adjoining fountains, I stopped to quench my thirst, rinse my handkerchief and pat the sweat prickling up on the back of my neck.

One fountain stood unadorned, with no signs or instructions hanging from its grey metal front. On a post above the other hung a cardboard sign: COLORED WATER.

"Cool," I said aloud. I bent over and pushed the button, curious to see what color water would spurt out of it.

Rough hands grabbed the collar of my cotton shirt, pulling me away and jerking up my head. "Whatcha' think you doin', young lady? You cain't drink that water. That water is fer colored folks, not white persons like us. Don't ya know how to read?"

Although the man was old and grizzly, he was not a tramp. But this guy scared me anyway, and he also made me angry. Why couldn't I have colored water, instead of plain old clear water? And what color was it, anyway? "Life is sure unfair," I thought as I moved to the other fountain, took a drink and stomped off towards the theater.

No one would claim that Chicago was less racist than Miami in the 1950s, but it was more latent, less obvious, perhaps more insidious. ◆

CHAPTER 7

A Scripted Life

THE ROTATING TABLE FAN STOOD SOFTLY HUMMING, impotent against the heat and humidity of a Miami August. We irrationally longed for the frigid winters of Chicago, the very weather my father had come here to escape in hopes of prolonging his hold on life. He sat on the couch, a shadow of his former self, wearing only his boxers and T-shirt. My two teenage brothers, about to start new schools, stood before him in mock attention. Good boys—still respectful even as they prepared to take on responsibilities meant for older men.

My father started slowly, talking took more effort recently. "I think you should consider changing your last name—maybe shortening it. Gozansky could limit your professional and social options here in the south. It's a new start here, a perfect time to do it."

My brothers retorted in perfect unison, "No, we will carry your name." My father brightened. He looked at his two sons warmly and nodded his head with pride—totally ignoring my presence in the room.

"What about me?" I asked as I stepped forward until I was between him and my brothers. "Why didn't you ask me if I wanted to change my name?" I demanded to know.

He looked up impatiently studying me with his weakened eyes. They were heavily lidded and darkly ringed but still penetrating. "You...you will get married and take your husband's name, have his babies and he will protect and provide for you."

There it was, the blue print for my life laid out before me — my status, my dependency, and worse, the totality of my father's expectations for me.♦

Seeking Daddy

I pounded on the door again, shrieking, "Daddy, let me in. Please let me in. I know you are in there!" No answer. I struck the door again with all my might, so hard this time that my knuckles bled. "Daddy, please!"

No answer. There was never an answer.

I had traced him back to the old brownstone in downtown Montreal — the one where my family went for Passover each spring, driving from Chicago. I was far too young to realize that we had driven to another country. I could picture the grey limestone steps leading up to the shabby wooden door. It was brown, like the bricks that covered the front of the narrow two-story building. I could even picture Aunt Esther, squat and square, in a cotton house dress, wiping her pudgy hands on her soiled apron and scowling as we came up the steps.

AUNT ESTHER WAS my father's sister-in-law. She was married to his oldest brother, Kalman—a lawyer in his past life, before emigrating from Russia. He had sent for Esther's younger sister in Russia to come to Canada and be his bride, but Esther arrived instead. Neither Esther nor Kalman, who then sold rags from a horse-drawn wagon, was ever happy with the union. Esther disliked my dad even more—the baby of the family, the one who got to go to college, marry whom he loved and live in America.

> *Never quite sure she really wanted us there, I ran with my two brothers and my sister past her into the parlor, sinking into the overstuffed faux velveteen settee and sniffing the air. Every year it smelled the same—of onions and garlic, brisket roasting and potatoes boiling. We knew, too, that any minute Aunt Esther would walk into the parlor and give us chores to do before our cousins arrived for the Seder.*

> *So why did he choose the Montreal brownstone? Why did he run away and hide from me?*

I woke up in a clammy sweat; my chest was hot and my bed clothes were damp. I woke this way every morning after having this dream, disoriented at first and then terribly sad—deeply, heart—wrenchingly sad. My dad wasn't in Montreal. He didn't run away from me. He wasn't hiding out, unwilling to be a part of my life.

Although I was well aware of my father's long illness and severe depression over his dependence on my mother, at twelve years old I could only process his death from congestive heart failure in terms of its effect on me: abandonment. But I never stopped seeking daddy. I looked for him in every man to whom I was attracted—misjudging physical strength for mental toughness, mistaking good looks for goodness, and confusing passion for love. ◆

Dad, William Gozansky, as a young man growing up in Montreal, Canada (ca. 1918). His family emigrated across Europe from Sokólka, Poland in the early 1900s when he was a toddler. *The Carole J. Garrison Family Archive.*

THE CONSTANT COMPANION

Preface

It wasn't until I completed this collection, these excerpts from my life, that I realized who has walked the path ahead of me, bringing me along; has walked with me as a fellow traveler; and has walked behind me, pushing me ever further. ∎

CHAPTER 1

The Boarder

Mom found the small wooden box when she was packing to move from her condo in North Miami to an assisted living high-rise in Pompano Beach. It was full of memorabilia, including souvenirs from the Chicago World's Fair and some love notes from my dad, who had died many years earlier at the age of fifty-two. Most were apologies for some tiff they had over my maternal grandmother. We sat on my mother's bed, taking turns reading aloud from the yellowed sheets of cramped writing, sniffling, and occasionally letting big wet tears fall on the aging paper.

Mom folded the last letter and placed it back in the box, which sat between us. Then, smiling wistfully, she asked, "Did I ever tell you the story about falling in love with your father?"

'LL BE BACK IN TEN DAYS. Then I'll apply for citizenship." Gert stared up into those deep, soft brown eyes and wondered why he was sharing this plan with her. After all, he was a boarder in her mother's house and, as much as she harbored a secret crush on Bill, he was an older, still-married man who even had a daughter. Her mother, Bertha, true to form, was already busy matchmaking for the time when his divorce was final. She had plenty of younger girlfriends in need of a suitable catch.

Gert stepped back and watched Bill get into the taxi and leave Maxwell Street. She fumbled with her fingers for a minute, hoping the shine in her eyes would dry so she could walk back inside the house without her mother's keen eye scrutinizing her every expression. She was confused as to why his leaving bothered her. He was like a big brother, giving Gert rides to the movies and helping her with homework.

Bill lived with her family in an old brownstone on Chicago's east side, a neighborhood that changed ethnicity with the decades. The Irish and the Poles had moved on; now the houses had mezuzahs on the door jambs and Russian was spoken on the street as often as Yiddish and English. Rooms were rented sub rosa, some with three to five siblings squeezed together into one iron four-poster. The untaxed income supplemented the meager 1930s salaries of the taxi drivers, milkmen, glaziers, and factory workers that made up the bulk of the neighborhood's men folk.

Bertha liked Bill, and she disliked Bill. She liked that he was college-educated, a rare thing for the day. She liked that he had a steady job. She didn't like his offering her advice or paying attention to her eldest daughter, who was a good ten years his junior. Gertie had enough challenges—a crooked spine and burn scars covering thirty percent of her body, including her neck and one cheek. Bertha thought she had made it perfectly clear to Bill: no hanky-panky on his part. And surely she didn't need to tell sensible, shy Gertie that, even though Bill was handsome, he wasn't the man for her.

At first the days without Bill passed slowly. Gert sat in the dormer window staring down to the street, watching kids play tag,

Gert and Bill's wedding portrait, May 1936. Mom wanted
Chrysanthemums, her favorite, but grandma insisted high
society brides were all carrying Callow Lilies. Bertha won.
The Carole J. Garrison Family Archive.

kick the can, and jump rope. She had no clue why she felt lonely. When she visited with her girlfriends, they teased her about the handsome boarder living at her house and giggled at the bright red blush that crawled up Gert's neck. She would run home and hide in the bathroom. When she cried, she couldn't understand why.

By the end of the ten days, Bill's absence was bearable; in fact, Gert didn't believe he was ever coming back. She imagined that he had arrived in Montreal and reconciled with his wife and daughter. Girlfriends, especially her best friend, Dubbie, stopped teasing her—either because they felt guilty or because Gert had become more immune to their taunts. She got on with her life, while Bertha continued to plot which friend she would introduce to Bill when and if he returned from Montreal.

The phone rang at Dubbie's house. No one was more surprised than Gert when Dubbie's eyes widened and she handed over the phone. "It's for you."

"I'm home," the voice said. Gert let the phone fall from her hands, as a startled Dubbie grabbed it before it hit the floor. "I've got to go," Gert called over her shoulder, with one foot already out the door. Her friends watched, anxious and curious, as she took off at a steady stride toward her home. Her pace quickened from walking to running; occasionally she skipped and then full-out ran again. She made out a figure standing on the stoop in front of her house. She quickened her pace once more as his arms began to rise by his sides—inviting, welcoming. Gert could barely breathe, and her brain stopped working. All she could do was climb the front steps and move into those receptive arms.

The wedding dress was white satin, long and flowing. Bertha had copied it out of a New York brides' magazine. Gert argued for chrysanthemums—her favorite—but Bertha insisted on callow lilies, like the brides carried in the magazine. Bertha may have lost the best candidate for her matchmaking campaign, but she wasn't going to give in on everything.◆

CHAPTER 2

Holding Mother's Hand

NO WHEELCHAIR. I'm not going to be pushed around like a toddler," Mom said, her stooped frame silhouetted against the bright vista of mountains and blue skies of Window Rock, Arizona.

"Really, Mom. Don't be so stubborn. It'll be easier for us to cover the museum," I said, pushing a wheelchair in her direction.

"But I can walk. It's embarrassing," she replied.

Ignoring her protests, I clicked my tongue impatiently while helping her to sit down in the chair. The Navajo Nation Museum was a beautiful arts center, but it was very large, containing many galleries full of contemporary art and ethnic history. I wanted to explore it all but, after several days of slow going to accommodate mom's aging shuffle, I decided that using the wheelchair provided for guests was a great idea.

Mom smiled up at me, camouflaging her resignation to her plight. I patted her hand and smiled back. I wasn't giving in and, if she wouldn't cooperate, I wasn't offering any options. It was for her own good. We began our mobile tour in a portrait gallery. Stunned to see faces with the likenesses of Tibetan friends who lived half a planet away staring from the canvasses, I forgot about my mom and wandered off without her.

"Hey!" she called.

"Sorry Mom! Won't happen again," I said as I retrieved her.

I kissed her lightly on the cheek, apologized again. We moved to the galleries filled with artifacts of struggle, resistance, death and survival. The high vaulted ceilings sent beams of light down to the floor below. One beam illuminated my mother as she read famous Native American quotes that lined the desert-red walls.

"You should remember this one, young lady," she said, pointing to a short quote on a plaque above a bronze warrior standing over a dead grizzly: "Force, no matter how concealed, begets resistance. — Lakota."

"I'm not forcing you to use the wheelchair. I just want to make getting around easier for you."

"Hmmph."

Then I saw it — a Pueblo quote a few yards further along the wall: "Hold on to my hand, even if someday I'll be gone away from you." Mom saw it too and looked meaningfully up at me. I reached out my hand; she took it and pulled herself up. A museum guide took the wheelchair away. Mom pulled back her shoulders, looked around to see who might be watching and, letting me take her hand in mine, continued slowly through the exhibits with me.

I'm not sure if we covered every exhibit, but we saw enough. Mom had a good laugh when I had to park myself on a bench to catch my breath. We chatted easily face to face, which was better than looking at the top of her head while she sat in the chair. I was glad that she had resisted, reclaimed her independence.

I also discovered something else that day — not just her strength, but also her increasing vulnerability. Her hands, soft and plump, had always held mine — crossing a busy street,

Carole and Gert on vacation at the Navaho Reservation, Arizona, circa 2005. We roamed across Arizona and New Mexico visiting museums, and ancient Indian settlements on high plateaus, and stared down into the amazing abyss that is the grand canyon. *The Carole J. Garrison Family Archive.*

maneuvering through a crowded store, entering a classroom for the first time. But that day in the museum, it was I who held her hand in mine. It was my hand supporting her, reassuring her, protecting her.

What is life? It is the flash of a firefly in the night. It is the breath of a buffalo in the wintertime. It is the little shadow which runs across the grass and loses itself in the sunset. – Blackfoot.♦

CHAPTER 3

The Sewing Machine

SHE KNEW AS WELL AS WE DID—she shouldn't drive any-more. Hiring that "don't need to go to court" lawyer, who, for a fee fixed the accident and fines so that you could retain your driver's license, was a last-ditch attempt to save her waning free-dom. One more fender-bender later, my three siblings and I knew there was no choice—the license, the car, had to go. Mother and countless strangers were in great peril if we didn't act.

Mom didn't take it well. She was depressed, napped a lot, and complained. My brother hired her a car and driver for two afternoons a week. His attempt to pacify her yielded him no rewards. "What If I run out of orange juice" she argued. "And, more to the point," she whined, "What if I just want to go out. I'm only eighty-two and you're making me a prisoner."

Several years later she had an accident while visiting her newest great-grandchild in Baltimore. It wasn't the first time she had fallen. She fell in Moscow on a Russian river trip a year or so back and we took away her international travel privileges;

another well-intended denial of freedom by her ever loving, vigilant children. But this time was more serious. She broke four ribs, cracked others and landed in rehabilitation in an unfamiliar city up north. That was it! All four of us took turns camping out at our nephew's home so we could stay with her at the rehab center, and each of us arrived at the same conclusion. At minimum Mom had to be in an adult living community, preferably near to my eldest brother—her son the doctor.

How much time could she have left? She was 95. We pondered our options. The housing bubble had burst and her North Miami Beach condo was now worthless. However, adult living in the high rent district of Pompano Beach was every bit as pricey as ever. She had savings, and we could get a little from the condo sale—surely enough money to see her through her remaining years.

Mother didn't take our intervention well. She railed against this last assault on her autonomy, finding ways to blame her daughters-in-law for her further incarceration.

"Don't tell anyone," she confided in my daughter six weeks later, "But I really like this place." She had beaten all expectations—ours as well as hers—thriving in her new active environment. She took comfort that at ninety-five she still lived alone, in her own apartment, read a book or more a week, and sewed dresses for her great-grandkids, who wore them more like hugs than as fashion statements.

By the time she reached ninety-eight we had begun rotating visits so that one of us was there for a weekend or couple of days each month. The children of her departed friends also visited. They identified her as a living conduit to their deceased parents.

Before flying down for a visit, she phoned and insisted I rent a car; we needed to buy a jacket pattern. She had found a piece of blue, synthetic material in her closet and was determined not to waste it. She was equally determined to sew the jacket with minimal help from me.

"Mom, the material is ugly," I said when she showed me the piece of cloth. "Mom, you have a closet full of jackets. You don't need this." Undaunted, she set her jaw and pulled herself up from her chair. "Let's go," she said and pushed her walker meaningfully towards the door.

I laid the pattern out, not paying any attention to saving material for another project. Just get it cut out, I thought. Mom sighed, "You're wasting material, you're not being careful." My back ached. It had been awhile since I bent over a cutting table for any length of time. If it hurt me, what would it have done to her? Glad I was there to help, I ignored her concerns about the left over material and stuffed the scraps into the waste bin so she didn't have to see them again.

Before I left to catch my plane back north, I set up her sewing machine on the small dining room table that had served as my cutting board the day before. I found her basket of threads and notions and wished her luck with her project. Hugs, kisses, goodbyes and the door closed behind me. I know, I thought as I waited for the elevator, it's not going to happen, but what can I do?

I was home for a couple of weeks, the sewing project all but forgotten. A call from mom reminded me of the awful blue material and her task. "How's the jacket coming along?" I asked. "Oh that," she sighed, "I had to throw it away. It was frustrating me."

I would have really liked to ask for her sewing machine; it's a better one than mine. But I didn't. It didn't pose a threat to her or others. Taking it away would have just been another reminder of her inevitably shrinking world. "I'm sorry," I said instead. "That's okay," she said cheerily, "Like you said, I've got a ton of jackets in my closet. But now I have to get to my bridge game, so I'll talk to you later." Surprised, I heard the solid click of the receiver. Holding the silent phone in my hand, I pictured my ninety-eight year-old mother pushing her walker down the hall to join her bridge group—and smiled.◆

CHAPTER 4

A Crosstown Bus

WE'D LOVE FOR YOU TO STAY with us while your here, but Elliot needs the car for work. You'll have to take the bus to the hospital in the mornings. We can pick you up at night. That way grandma will be able to see the baby." My niece was pouring coffee with her left hand while trying to burp her infant with her right. I took the coffee pot and finished pouring coffee into the two mugs sitting on the counter." I nodded, taking a sip of my coffee, "Works for me, that's why mom was here after all, to greet her newest great grandson."

Waiting for the 9:10 a.m. cross-town bus for the first time, I stood in front of Starbucks in the chic neighborhood of Fells Point and squinted in the early morning sun. Across the street were a small upscale art gallery and a boutique with over-priced Indian clothes, bright over-sized cotton blouses and bohemian dresses with long skirts made of crinkly paisley material. In the distance, I could just make out the water sparkling in Baltimore's stylish inner harbor, which reflected from the windows of downtown skyscrapers.

When the bus arrived, I stepped up to the fare box realizing that I had no idea what a ride cost anymore.

"You a senior?" asked the driver, not waiting for my reply. "Fifty cents."

I didn't know whether I looked like a senior or if worrying about my mother's rehab had aged me more than I cared to admit. I put two quarters in the slot and moved to a blue plastic seat directly in front of the middle door. I could have sat any-where—the bus was empty save for me and an elderly gentleman holding a cane and wearing a World War II military cap.

The old man got off at the VA hospital. A sprinkling of others boarded in the downtown area, mostly black people looking tired, as if they had just finished working the night shift. As we moved through Baltimore's east side and along its famous row houses—a few remodeled, many more abandoned and most in need of repair—the bus began to fill. Almost to a person, the newer riders looked at me with a hint of surprise, found a seat and then ignored me. Before getting off, they turned to look at me again.

Passing more boarded-up brownstones, burned-out storefronts and soul food takeouts, the bus eventually entered Baltimore's mostly white suburbs. Only a few passengers remained when I arrived at my destination, the Sinai Medical and Rehabilitation Center, a forty-five-minute ride from my nephew's condo.

On the second morning, the ride passed much like it had the day before, except that some of my fellow riders nodded shyly to me as if I had become an acquaintance. Although I returned their nods, I strangely felt like a sociologist doing ethnographic research in an unfamiliar culture.

By the third morning, as the nods expanded to smiles, one woman came right out and asked, "Honey, whatcha' doin' on this bus?" The man next to me stopped talking to god while he waited for my answer.

"My mother, she's frail, in her nineties. She's in the Sinai rehab hospital recovering from a fall. Cracked ribs and some other stuff.

I go to keep her company." I didn't add that I had no car because I'd flown up from Kentucky. The passengers' interest gave me comfort, a sense of belonging. I didn't want to appear arrogant.

There was a chorus of ah hums and a few amens, accompanied by a lot of sympathetic head shaking.

On the fourth day, my bus ride was free because the coin machine was broken. Rather than taking the impaired bus entirely off-line, it operated on a random schedule so that no one knew if or when it would arrive. Everyone who finally boarded acted as if he or she had won a lottery, me included. The bus hummed with a feeling of good fortune and a sense of anticipation that the next day might also be lucky. The other passengers included me in their sense of well-being, in their high fives and wide grins.

For the next several days, I was greeted as a member of the bus community—often asked how my mother was doing or offered prayers for her recovery. I stopped making judgments, and I quit assuming that a disheveled man was a drunk or that a woman struggling with two toddlers and an infant was a welfare mother. I stopped recoiling from the mumbling man, as well as the slicked-haired teenager in low-rider jeans and his multi-pierced girlfriend. I returned smiles with smiles, embraced by this slice of caring humanity who journeyed with me every day.

My mother healed a week or so later. When she was released from the rehab center, my brother came to take her home to Miami. My bus rides ended. I didn't say goodbye to the daily riders; I didn't even think of them as I flew home to get my car, return to work and resume my everyday bus-less life. And yet, over the past fifteen years, I have found myself fondly remembering my fellow travelers and our brief encounters. I carry with me their kindness, and I thank them for their lessons in humanity.

Life's lessons do not come from books; they come from open hearts. They come when we understand that our common struggles are shared amongst us all—those who ride the bus, and those who don't. ♦

CHAPTER 5

The Little Red Suitcase

THE PHONE RANG AND A FEW MOMENTS later my daughter was tapping my shoulder softly but insistently. The window was dark save for a thin magenta line stretching across the horizon. I had been waiting for the call.

"It was Uncle David. GG is gone."

"Okay, I'll book the airline tickets," I grunted, turned over and pulled the covers back over my head.

She was struggling to push down the handle of the small red suitcase so that she could stuff it under the seat in front of her. The woman standing in the aisle tapped her foot impatiently, waiting to take her seat. But Gertrude was nervous and focused on her task. Finally, the handle down, she shoved the bag with her feet until it fit snugly and tightly. She didn't want the flight attendant fussing at her if it stuck out in the aisle.

Gert, 2013. *Bill Gozansky Photography, LLC.*

Gert turned and smiled up at the impatient woman who, with an unnecessarily loud sigh, collapsed into her seat with a soft thud. They tussled a bit to find the right seat belts and then settled down to hear the safety briefing. Gert especially liked, "Put on your own oxygen mask first before helping others." She thought that was good advice for living life.

Her attention turned to her surroundings. She noted with satisfaction the extra leg room, the video console above the closed lunch tray, and a recent People magazine rather than a boring in-flight publication. Gert also noticed the little red bag peeking out from under the row in front of her. The bag had gone along with her on many travels—to the Himalayas, the Near East, the Far East, the Middle East, and even to Africa and the Galapagos Islands. It always contained her medications, fiber for travelers' constipation, a clean pair of undies and a spare pair of glasses, as well as a book or two. Her great-grandkids always recognized it when she came to visit; after all, it was a kids-size suitcase, which made them giggle. Gert really liked it, and the bag made her feel independent because she could take it anywhere without any help. Her favorite travel motto was: Don't take more than you can carry.

The woman in the next seat sighed again, so Gert offered her a Tic Tac from the little plastic case she took from her purse. The woman accepted, putting the small candy between her two pudgy fingers and giving Gert a small smile to match the size of the mint. But Gert considered this a positive sign and leaned in to speak.

"This journey has taken me a lifetime," she confided. The woman sighed yet again, although her smile was *slightly warmer. They traveled side-by-side for the rest of the flight in silence.*

Gert fell into step with the throngs of passengers filing out of the plane and began the long walk toward the exit. Ignoring the people lined up along the route, Gert walked on—her shoes clicking softly beneath her, her little red bag rolling behind her.

Always hoping but never really expecting it, she heard a familiar voice calling her name. It was familiar in that odd kind of way that you recognize but haven't heard for a long, long time. She heard it again: "Gert." And then, stronger and more insistent, "Gerty!" She definitely knew that voice. She looked up at the crowd of people lining the path to the exit and there he was—with his arms outstretched, looking just like he did when they had been in their prime of life before she had lost him to heart failure all those forty-five years ago.

"I've been waiting for you," he said as he took her hand in his. "Our hearts never failed each other." Then he took the little red suitcase in his other hand, "And you won't need this anymore."

The sun streaming brightly through my window woke me the second time that morning. My mother, GG, was dead at ninety-nine years of age. She was on her last journey and it was okay."♦

CHAPTER 6

Walking with Mom

WALKING IN THE BRIGHT GLARE of the rising sun, it wasn't difficult to be transported thirty years back to when mom and I took early morning walks together. I saw her in my mind's eye, her hands loosely clasped behind her back. I teased her about that, now I walk the same way. The setting was different, instead of blocks of pastel colored cement block condos surrounded by manicured lawns and designer landscaping, all smelling of chlorine, I'm walking along a narrow road lined with a riot of lush tropical greenery, so thick I can't see the houses that lay beyond. Instead of the cooing of morning-doves and the chirping of sparrows, I hear the harsh caterwauling of peacocks, and even catch sight of an albino peahen. The steamy Florida air sinks into my bones as I walk—and think of her.

Escaping Ohio's frigid temperatures, I would visit over winter break, mother my age now, and me, middle aged and still needing my mother's care and Florida's healing climate. She would cook my favorite foods, make coffee with a hint of cinnamon before I woke so it was ready when I padded out to the living room. We would nap together in her bed, holding hands while we slept. Sometimes I would find her asleep on the couch instead, covered with my grandmother's afghan—I felt abandoned when she did, as if she left me to nap with her mother.

I know she is not under the neatly trimmed lawns at Mt. Nebo cemetery. She's with my dad, finally able to share their eternal peace together. Still, I didn't think this week would be so hard.◆

BLINDSPOTS

Preface

According to literary experts, Arnold Lobel's children's story, "Frog and Toad Together: A List," was simply a tale about friendship in which the plot device, a list of things to do, had a finite beginning and ending. For me, however, the story illustrates the value of the checklist itself—a slip of paper that organizes daily life and reminds us of the tasks we need to accomplish as distractions bombard us.

Not only does the To Do List often contain and give importance to the day's minutiae, but it also helps us to keep track of our A List chores. Feelings of pride and satisfaction accompany penciling through a task; stress and anxiety lessen as we place a check mark in the margin. I am an inveterate list maker; I made lists long before I could blame my poor memory on senior moments.

Occasionally however, I awake from a string of vague, mildly distressing dreams . . . and face an uncomfortable truth.

We are simply never "done" with the task of raising children. ■

CHAPTER 1

Awakening to the Dream

I READ SOMEWHERE ONCE that we try our damnedest as parents to squash the very qualities our children need to be successful adults.

Red-faced with clenched hands, she shouted, "I hate you. I hate you." Her words changing the living room into a chasm of anger neither of us could cross.

"But I love you," I whimpered, as a mixture of anguish and anger swirled like a tempest in my brain.

This was my child, my first born—this snarling, gangly fourteen-year-old monster—who was screaming at me. What? Why? I was smart enough to know that I wasn't the first mother to hear this. I had thought the same thing about my mother a time or two during my adolescence, but this behavior was decidedly over the top!

She had just been arrested for shoplifting and, to make matters worse, assaulting a police officer. Debra was born six feet tall, or at least it felt like that trying to pick her up as a toddler or having to stand on a stool to hug her by the time she was twelve. I had all kinds of excuses for her, for me. There was the divorce, and the fact that she looked so much like her father I could hardly bear to look at her; often I misplaced my anger at her rather than where it belonged. Then there was the move, becoming a cop in Atlanta, another move and earning a Ph.D. By the time she was fourteen, I had dragged her from Miami to Atlanta to Columbus, turned her into a latch-key child and basically ignored her, hoping she would manage to grow up while I was growing up on my own.

Her IQ hovering around 174, she read and understood Shakespeare at the age of six. If that wasn't challenging enough to a parent, she thought in equations; I had stopped taking math classes after failing eighth-grade algebra. All children, including little ones, understand fairness. Debra got the concept early on, and we became strangers who inhabited the same physical plane but not the same emotional space.

Debra's latest and most overt acting out couldn't have come at a worse time, as if there is ever a better time for your child to make real your worst fears about her. Never mind that she had cooked my live-in boyfriend's tropical fish while we were away camping with her younger sister for the weekend. Never mind that she looked stoned half of the time and, as I found out later, she was. At the point in time she had committed her worst indiscretion, I was preparing for my comprehensive exams for my Ph.D. in Public Administration with an emphasis in Corrections.

Perhaps it was my classes in Juvenile Justice; maybe it was the powerful images from dystopian movies of the day, like the 1976 film, *Logan's Run;* possibly my dream was an intervention from the Universe.

"Debra, cooperate," I pleaded, as the authorities came for her as they did for all children on their sixteenth birthday.

Society had become quite insensitive to the plight of humanity, especially among young people whose indifference to human suffering rose to the level of national policy. The experts said, "The solution is simple; we will maim children, temporarily of course, so that they will experience helplessness and develop a sense of empathy and sympathy for others less fortunate."

Debra, tall and powerfully built, was having none of this psycho-babble torture. She would not go quietly into the operating room.

"Debra, it's for your own good," I coaxed. "All children have this done; it will be quick and, in less than four months, the cast will be off and you'll be good as new."

"I won't; you can't make me," she screamed at me and the orderlies who were trying to get her to calm down. She tore at her white hospital gown and tried unsuccessfully to bolt from their control. The other teenagers waiting their turn watched this rebellion anxiously, as did their parents. Terrified of what the government would do if she did not go through with the procedure, I stood back as the bigger of the two orderlies handcuffed her to the wheelchair and proceeded through the big electronic doors as they opened and swallowed everyone up in the bright overhead lights of the operating theater.

I followed meekly behind. The government had been doing this for several years now, claiming huge success in behavior modification as it attempted to engineer a kinder, gentler society. But the rebellion was not squashed, and Debra thrashed and howled on the operating table. She had to be further restrained after lunging for the surgeon and practically toppling her over. Reinforcements were called in—more nurses, bigger and stronger orderlies and another surgeon.

"Screw it," the second surgeon said. If she won't lie still, just do it." Then I heard the bone in her leg shatter.

"I'm sorry, Mrs. Garrison. We tried for a clean break, but she just kept moving. The bone is shattered, and I doubt she will ever walk without a limp again. If only she was better behaved," he chided.

Months later, the cast removed, my rebellious daughter hadn't morphed into the sensitive, empathic youngster promised by the government but into something very different. No longer the tall, haughty, powerful young girl, she walked stooped with her chin low to her chest and her foot-dragging as she limped along.

I woke as if shot by some unknown dart of adrenalin. I was cold and clammy; my eyes were wide with shock and fright. It was a nightmare, just a bad dream, I told myself as I tried to calm my pounding heart. I wanted Debra to change and meet my expectations, not to break her. Yes, yes, that's what I wanted—a daughter who was strong and powerful but who used those traits in a way that conformed to my ideals rather than to clash against my every wish.

I approached Debra's adolescent angst with renewed commitment, but it did not end for several more years, no matter what we tried. Finally, maturation, boarding school and a year of following a Grateful Dead national tour moderated her enough to turn what was a troubling and difficult teenager to grow up into a creative and successful person. It was full of bumps along the way, but intellect and risk-taking trumped poor parenting and life's challenges.

I learned something that night and in years of subsequent sleepless nights that has stuck with me as vividly as the night I first had that dream. All of the traits children possess that allow them to act out and challenge our norms are the very characteristics they need to navigate the swells and eddies of adulthood. Our job as adults is not to subdue emotionally or physically our children into obedience, but instead to champion their will.◆

CHAPTER 2

Bourgeoisie

"MOM, I FOUND a dress for the wedding!"

It was good to hear the excitement in Debra's voice, though I wondered how much it would cost me. Nevertheless, she appeared committed to staying within a pretty conservative budget for the entire affair—less than the cost of some women's trousseau.

> *Funny, I had thought that Debra, a counterculture groupie who had followed the Grateful Dead around the country for a year, didn't know what a trousseau was.*

"A dress? Great. What does it look like? Does it come with a veil? White? Ivory?" I asked, trying not to hint at any dollar concerns.

Debra's wedding at the top of Mt. Stowe, New Hampshire, 1985. She wore a newly pur-
chased Jessica McLintock ivory lace mid-calf length dress and kissed her husband as the
wind blew streamers of colored crape-paper out over the mountain peak. *The Carole J.
Garrison Family Archive.*

"At the Goodwill store on the island. Isn't that awesome? Mom? Mom, are you there?"

My stomach lurched. "A Goodwill shop?"

"Yeah. Lucky, right?"

Before I could stop myself, I said, "You are not getting married in a dress from Goodwill."

Debra was a beautiful bride in her ivory lace Jessica McClintock sheath and ivory leather booties. I dabbed at my eyes as she and Jeff stood on top of Mount Stow, surrounded by multi-colored banners waving like flags in the breeze. Determined to enjoy my daughter's happiness, I tried not to notice that the young man performing the ceremony bore an uncanny resemblance to the singer Meat Loaf.

I'd like to think that I suffered "mommy muscle spasms" over the news of a dress from Goodwill, but of course they weren't. They were the convulsions of a bourgeoisie.◆

CHAPTER 3

No Choice is Free

I LAY DOWN NEXT TO HER in Marta's guest room on the double bed. We arrived two days earlier in Louisville from my daughter's home in Richmond, Kentucky. It was Louisville or Baltimore and I had Marta, an old friend and colleague, in Louisville. The bright yellow comforter was the same as the one that my daughter had in her room for years. That is, until she decided to express herself and picked out a dark brown and red one. Still, I think it was oddly comforting to us both to be under a familiar blanket in this otherwise unfamiliar apartment waiting for—what? Salvation? Doom?

Seeing the roundness of her tummy as she lay on her back, I felt ill for a moment and had to struggle to regain my composure. Did she feel anything? Was she trapped? Had I trapped her into doing this, without giving her any other reasonable option? I couldn't take her home pregnant without causing a huge amount of angst in the family. If I did, how would we keep the toxic, bad boyfriend-father out of her life? There were no more Florence Crittenton adoption homes, which had been popular into the 1960s, where I could send her until the baby was born. I was convinced that this was a clean solution—the right thing to do, what sensible people do.

She has not even bothered to read the instructions given to her for today's appointment. She's holding a bottle of water and is complaining of being hungry. I tell her to call the clinic. I remember the little sign over the water fountain in the waiting room reminding patients not to drink or eat anything after midnight on the day of the procedure. She pulls a small square of paper from her pocket with these same instructions. She is also to bring several large pads and a bathrobe. She asks, "What kind of pads—like tampons?"

"No, not tampons," I tell her. "Maxi pads—like pads for your period."

I borrow an Omni Hotel bathrobe from Marta's bathroom and we leave an hour early, heading to the Save More market to get sanitary pads. We are relieved that the snowfall has just been a dusting, so the streets are clear.

We don't speak on the way to the clinic, except for one awkward moment when she turns to me and asks, "Do you like the name Aiden? We were going to call him Aiden, if it was a boy. We didn't pick a girl's name."

My head jerks, and I try to choke back my anger. Drawing a breath, I realize this is the first hint that she is thinking about the pregnancy rather than the procedure. Still, I hiss, "When you are pregnant as an independent, functioning adult, I will be joyous; but we're not going there now."

"What ev," she says, turning back to stare out the car window. We arrive at the clinic at 9:15 a.m. and plow our way through the throng of protesters, whom we had faced the day before. Then, they had intimidated us—today, they were just annoying. Protesters don't offer prenatal care; they don't acknowledge the agony of making the decision to terminate a pregnancy. They warn of hell in the next life without offering to help anyone in this life.

It is now after 11:00 am, and we are still waiting for the doctor to arrive. I feel nauseous and hungry at the same time. We wait. My daughter, who is fiddling with her laptop, is frustrated and angry. We wait.

It's now 11:15 am. Finally, her name is called. I trip as I stand up to hug her. Her eyes are cold, and her hand goes out to stop me. No hug. She takes her bag and heads to the surgical area.

I cross the street to the Subway outlet, buy an egg sandwich and a small black coffee, and pee. I pee a lot when I'm nervous. I've been peeing every twenty minutes or so. My brother Nat calls. We talk. He is calm, supportive. I notice that my hands are shaking a little bit, and the old familiar hole between my upper back and spleen is opening.

I put more quarters in the parking meter. It seems to use them up faster than it should.

I return to the clinic's waiting room. I take it as a good sign that she is still in with the doctor. For a while, I just sit. I fear her coming out and saying that the doctor—or she—couldn't go through with it. When she doesn't appear, I know that it is happening. I wait; my hands are getting cold; the hole in my chest is growing emptier or bigger. I can't tell.

The long wait is wearing on everyone else as well. Friends and relatives of the patients play with cell phones, bounce their knees, or read two-year-old *People* and *Glamour* magazines. It's deadly silent until one person says, "Damn. Did you hear what those protesters were shouting?" Suddenly people across the room are talking to each other, muttering into the space that both divides us and connects us, and reaching out for affirmation, for some sense of community. One young man complains loudly, "Do those protesters think we just woke up this morning and decided to go for an abortion? We've struggled and agonized over this decision for weeks."

"Line up at the window," a nurse calls from behind her little glass window. "I will give you approximate release times. They may not be exact, but don't worry about it. Sometimes the procedure takes a little longer for some women than for others." I get in line for my daughter's time. It will be another fifty minutes. I am relieved, as we will make it to my home in West Virginia by late afternoon.

More quarters. Do I need more quarters? Several people show me the rolls of them clutched in their hands and ask if I have enough. "Thanks. I think I'm fine," I say and return to my seat. It gets really quiet again. I need to pee.

The door to the surgical area opens, and I see my daughter peering out. She looks pale and sullen; she's holding her stomach. Relief washes away the fear and fills up the cavity in my chest. I move towards her and say, "Do you need to sit for a minute?"

"No. Let's get out of here."

I reach for the door handle of the lobby, but she brushes by me saying, "Mom, I'm not a cripple." I walk behind her to the car. As I put the key in the ignition, I can't help but wish that she would sleep throughout the four-hour trip home.

This is the story of any mother who has a twenty-something daughter in this social-network, culture-driven society. But it is my story, and my daughter got involved with the wrong boy, landed in an abusive relationship, and made some very bad choices. Panic, anger, fear, and grief all flood back with the retelling of it.

Pregnancy should be joyous, but pregnancy is not a life. A life is a child born into a loving family—into a society that supports, not scorns its plight when things go wrong or need extra support to thrive. Our society confuses "right to life" with "right to suffer for the sins of the parent."

The choice to terminate a pregnancy is an agonizing dilemma, but sometimes the most caring people are required to make that choice.◆

CHAPTER 4

A Promise Made, a Promise Kept

It's easy to become an ordained minister," said the web-site. "Just go online to any Universal Life Church and click our 'Get Ordained' button." Although I wasn't convinced that this was the answer to the problem, I clicked the button anyway. Thirty-five dollars later, charged to my Visa card, I was an ordained minister with credentials, a parking sticker and a PDF containing an array of wedding ceremonies to choose from. The irony of my ordination—I, a sworn secular humanist of Jewish origin—was not lost on family or friends.

M Y ADOPTED DAUGHTER TEVI was born a Buddhist, a birthright from her mother. Her name in fact means "Angel of Buddha." It wasn't that she was a practicing Buddhist; she had even attended a Catholic school, which provided a gentle and protective environment for this café au lait-skinned beauty of uncertain academic skills. But she had adopted neither Christianity nor Judaism as a spiritual home. Her betrothed, Lloyd, came from a family of devout Missionary Baptists. Tevi and Lloyd's daughter, Liza, was almost one year old but, despite the congregation's desire to support the young couple, the minister of Lloyd's evangelical Christian church refused to marry them unless Tevi converted to his faith.

"Why didn't you buy Lloyd a birthday present?" Tevi demanded at breakfast a few weeks before I discovered I could become ordained and perform a legal wedding ceremony.

"You tell Lloyd that when you're married and he's my son-in-law, he'll be on my gift list. Until then, *nada*."

"Fair enough," Tevi said, with surprisingly good humor. "But how will we get married? His pastor won't perform the ceremony."

Her humor was a welcome change from the tension between us that arose with her announcement that she was pregnant, keeping the baby and not yet ready to consider marriage. My reaction had been outrage. I was livid. In stony coldness, I had brought Tevi to tears by telling her that I did not save her from a perilous life in Cambodia so that she could become an unwed mother in America. It took months of coaxing to get her to talk to me after that encounter.

Friends were sympathetic, they encouraged me to step back and take a more understanding view of the situation. They sent messages of congratulations on Tevi's pregnancy. It could be worse, they claimed. They knew about Tevi's severe malnutrition as a toddler in the orphanage that had left her cognitively impaired, and although capable with concrete tasks and clever social conversation, she had not finished the GRE—reading simply overwhelmed her. What were her possibilities in life? Lloyd was not a druggie or an alcoholic; he was in college, had a job, loved Tevi and had accepted paternity immediately. Give them a chance.

Finally, resigned to the inevitable, I conceded, Tevi was happy, maybe the happiest she had ever been. I had no right to take away her joy. Shame on me for using her vulnerability to bring her to tears, to regret her decisions. I shouldn't impose my expectations on her. No, my job was to be there for her and help her to live her life joyously, on her own terms.

"You can convert if you want," I said. It's okay with me. But don't do it if it's not what you want."

Her elbows on the table, Tevi leaned her face on her fists. "I don't want to. Help me."

I got ordained, but I was leaving the country for a couple of months. If they were to marry before Liza's first birthday, it had to happen now. With barely time to buy Tevi a dress and some pretty costume jewelry, the ceremony was held in the city park less than two weeks later. Out-of-towners, the bulk of my family, had no chance to attend. My son-in-law, Tim, gave the bride away; my granddaughter, Ella, was the flower girl; and my middle daughter, Samantha, held baby Liza while her parents stood before me. Squeezed into a black dress (over a spandex bodysuit) that I considered appropriate for a minister, I read from a modified Buddhist ceremony that was included in my ministerial package. Lloyd's extended family was in attendance, grouped in a circle around us.

"Kynome sroline, Tevi," I whispered in the middle of the ceremony. Lloyd heard me but didn't understand what I'd said, nor did he comprehend Tevi's and my reaction. Tears welled up in her eyes; my own tears spilled over and ran down my cheeks. Today was both the end and the beginning of a long uphill journey that had begun years ago, in an orphanage in Phnom Penh. I had adopted a little girl to give her a chance at life—today I was keeping that promise.

When the ceremony concluded, the witnesses and I signed the marriage certificate. Tevi left with Lloyd's family for a reception at his parent's home in rural Ohio; Lloyd left to return to work. Samantha, Tim, Ella and I went to a new restaurant for dinner.

"What did you say in the middle of the ceremony?" Samantha wanted to know.

"Kynome sroline, Tevi. I love you, Tevi." And I do.♦

Carole and granddaughter Ella ready for Tevi's wedding. *The Carole J. Garrison Family Archive.*

CHAPTER 5

Rite of Passage

"MOM, I NEED YOU. I need you now." Samantha, my daughter, called down from the door leading to my apartment from her part of the house we shared. Her voice was shrill and loud. My first thought was that she had cut herself cooking dinner. Nevertheless, clad only in PJ bottoms and braless under a light sweater, I started up the stairs.

"Will...he's been in a car accident. He's all right; he called me. I need to get him, but I don't think I can drive."

"It's okay," I said, retreating to grab my purse and slip on some shoes.

Sam sat next to me while Ella, age nine, cowered in the backseat. "Don't hit anyone," Sam said as we drove away on our neighborhood's narrow lane. I slowed down as we passed a strolling couple out walking their dog and, gaining some mental control, turned onto the main road leading to the city of Milton and to Will.

The distance to Milton seemed endless, not the short eight miles it really was, and every traffic light stayed red for an eternity. Sam clicked her nails and, in some dread silence, imagining her mother's fears. My own chest began to tighten and dark thoughts filled my mind.

"Do you know where he is in Milton? He must be on the right-hand side of the road if he was driving to work. Call him," I insisted.

The slow passage of time pressed in on me, and I was anxious to know where we would find him. All he had told his mom was near downtown Milton. Sam started calling. "He doesn't answer. Why doesn't he answer his damn phone?" She tried several more times, with no response.

Each time I heard Will's voicemail message, the emptiness in my chest expanded. Sam's voice got shakier, shriller; her nails clicked against each other incessantly.

Finally, we could see blue, white and red emergency lights swirling up ahead, as well as three or four sheriff's cars and the rear of an ambulance.

My own breath left me as I told Sam to breathe. "That must be him!" she cried. Horrific thoughts that Will had gone into shock or even had a heart attack filled me with dread. As I pulled up behind the squad cars, we could see the passenger side of Will's van crumpled against a tree, with its engine exposed and the fender on the ground.

The ambulance began pulling away. Sam—pale and shaking, driven by fear and anxiety—leapt from the car and ran...until I lost sight of her behind the cluster of vehicles. Ella remained crouched in the back seat. Leaving her there, I ran to the scene.

"Where's the boy?" I shouted to the officers, who were standing in a group. "Back there," they replied, pointing. Not in the ambulance! My brain clicked and my chest closed, the terrible evisceration suddenly subsiding. I went around to the far side of the van, where Samantha and an EMT nurse sat on either side of Will. I stroked his red hair, but he barely noticed me.

Will suffered a broken finger, a loss of self-esteem and the night off from work. Recalling my own new-driver accident as well as those of my three daughters, I wanted to believe these accidents were simply a rite of passage, a checked box in the columns of our lives. No, I knew that was just a ploy to fend off fear. We had lucked out in the lottery of life's unexpected sharp left turns. The earth still revolved on its axis. Will was safe and whole.♦

DETOURS

Preface

My decade-old college degree in Soviet government and Russian history prepared me for few if any upscale careers. Without the thighs to be a successful waitress, or the math skills to work at a bank, I had few choices. Fueled initially by anger and a desire to emasculate my soon-to-be ex-husband, I applied to the Atlanta Police Department in the turbulent early 1970s. My job as an officer was both a detour from the false security of suburban housewife and mother roles and a starting point for a very different life. ■

CHAPTER 1

Bloody Palms

I HAD BEEN IN UNIFORM ONLY a few weeks when I tripped and fell, hands splayed, and slid across the loose stones and asphalt just outside the gate surrounding the Atlanta Bureau of Police headquarters. My hands burned like they were on fire. As I crouched there for a minute, hoping that the stinging would subside, two highly polished black wingtips and a pair of navy blue pant legs appeared in front of me.

"Officer Garrison."

I let my gaze follow the pant legs up until I could crane my neck enough to see the stern face of Atlanta's police chief staring down at me. "Sir," I said, struggling to get to my feet.

His eyes narrowed, his voice was hard. "Garrison, police officers don't cry."

Rivulets of blood began to seep across my palms.

"Oh no? Watch me."♦

CHAPTER 2

Policewoman: Circa 1970s

"I WISH YOU HAD LET ME GO TO VIETNAM and become a war hero," Franklin whined during one of the arguments leading up to the dissolution of our nine-year marriage. I muttered under my breath, "If I had known what a prick you are, I would have gladly let you go."

In 1973, the lawyers congratulated me after Florida's no fault divorce hearing. I was emancipated—a single mother of two thrust into the world with a decade-old college degree in Soviet government and secondary education. Unable to eat more than a cup of Cream of Wheat at mealtime, I was thin, small-boned and certainly not gifted in sports. But I was determined to move on with my life and prove myself a "better man" than my ex-husband.

I would never have thought about joining the police force on my own. I couldn't remember ever engaging in a physical fight, ever touching a gun. Although I had harbored secret dreams of being an avenger when I was little, I had left them behind ages ago. It was a former policewoman, director of the Miami-Dade women's detention center and a mentor of sorts, who encouraged me to go into policing because the federal government had just passed the Law Enforcement Administration Act.

The LEAA was a response to the public outcry against the police in the aftermath of student protests at the 1968 Democratic convention in Chicago. Among other provisions, it reimbursed active police officers who enrolled in college. I packed up my daughters and moved to Atlanta. The city's police department, under a consent decree, was hiring women and minorities.

Although I barely met the age limit of thirty-two, I had a college degree when applicants needed only a high school GED. What I lacked was the required height — 5'9" — the average height for a male. But a Pennsylvania woman had just won a discrimination suit against a local police department for its height requirement and, within months of the decision, Atlanta had revised its own requirements. The woman in Pennsylvania never became a police officer, but I walked through the door that she had opened.

Having met the basic requirements, I then had to pass a rigorous physical agility test that included four chin-ups. Even though women in general have much less upper-body strength than men, I personally had never even carried my own groceries to the car much less worked out at a gym. I didn't even own a pair of sweatpants. So I put up a metal bar across the top of each doorway in my apartment and, every day for six weeks, I jumped and pulled myself up until — my hands covered in raw blisters — I could manage three consecutive chin-ups. I would have to rely on adrenalin to do the fourth one.

"Can I wear gloves?" I asked my recruiter. "My hands are blistered and I'm afraid that, when I grab the metal bar, the pain will keep me from holding on." He probably thought I meant weight-lifting gloves, as he agreed to allow them. Clueless about the proper attire, however, I meant white cotton opera gloves.

Atlanta Bureau of Police Services, 1976 Annual Report. When I wasn't practicing chin ups I wrote the annual report and staged the cover photo for the bicentennial, of the Declaration of Independence. *The Carole J. Garrison Family Archive.*

Police Cadet 1974, Atlanta Bureau of Police Services. Skirts and high heels were the uniform of the day, "a la" TV's popular show, *Police Woman.* I led the protests to let women wear uniforms like our male colleagues. It took a few more years to get ones that fit. *The Carole J. Garrison Family Archive.*

The day of my test, wearing a lavender mini-skirt, a snap-crotch blouse and white go-go boots to match the gloves—the uniform of suburban housewives in the early 1970s—I pulled myself up three times before hanging on the bar, like a sack of potatoes, for what seemed to be an eternity. No adrenalin pumped to my rescue. Unable to move, I was convinced that I'd failed the test. Then, without warning, the lieutenant giving the exam put his hand under my skirt. No other motivation was necessary as my body reflexively jerked upward and completed its fourth pull-up.

Postscript: Despite my ignominious start, I was a quick learner, graduating at the top of my academy class and eventually earning a distinguished service medal from the department. I also made use of the LEAA's tuition reimbursement program. Attending graduate school at night, I obtained a Master of Public Administration degree and was accepted to Ohio State University's doctoral program in the same field.

During my four years as a policewoman, I had been forged anew in a crucible of brutality, sexism and racism. But patrol was a young person's game and, at the age of thirty-six, it was too late for me to move up the ranks in Atlanta's male-dominated department—making it almost impossible to effect change from within. With my anger over the divorce moderated and the need to prove myself a better man mollified, I left Atlanta for Ohio State. Although I wasn't sure of my final destination, I knew that there was more for me to do in the world, and I was eager to discover what lay ahead.

When I joined the department in the 1970s, not a single woman held a rank above patrol officer. But in 1994, Beverly Harvard—an African-American woman who signed up during my stint—became Chief of Police.♦

CHAPTER 3
The VIP

WE'RE ALL RECKLESS, aren't we? I like to think so, at least while we were young, somewhere between child and adult. My recklessness extended far beyond those limits, or more likely, I came to adulthood late. My text book suburban married life had come crashing down, leaving me agoraphobic, with two children and a desperate wish to escape the man whose last words to me were, "The sex wasn't bad, but your tits are small," followed by, "and you stopped me from going to Vietnam, you stole my manhood."

At 21, I had left my mother's home to play house and live according to my script. I'd be damned before going back to my mother's, and even worse, staying around to watch my ex and his new wife pick up my children on the weekends. Instead, I packed up my kids, and fled to Atlanta, Georgia and tried to do something totally off the reservation. I became a cop.

My round top, navy blue hat always slipped down on my forehead making it look like I was wearing my big brother's uniform. In fact, everything about the police uniform was too big and ill fitting. My shiny patent leather Sam Brown belt and holster were enormous, and the 48 Smith and Wesson, that hung awkwardly from my hip felt heavy and huge. But, I was a cop—an Atlanta Police Bureau officer, my silver badge, and radio attached to my shirtfront with trepidation and pride. I had never seen a gun before becoming an officer, never experienced a physical tussle. I hadn't been a bad cop—sometimes I had been a great cop, but I was a female in the 1970's, surviving by wits not brawn, brains not muscle.

The door to the captain's office was open. I overheard him talking to two officers, one standing attentively, the other slouching and holding a pinched cigarette butt in between his fingers. "The Congresswoman will need to be picked up from the airport and taken to the hotel. She has about two hours from landing at Hartsfield and giving her speech to the Urban League."

"Really, Cap! Who's gonna hurt Shirley Chisholm? Besides, what if the Urban League sends their own greeters?"

"You don't want this gig? Fine...I'll send someone else."

Before they could utter their words of contrition and take the assignment, I stepped into the office. "I'll do it."

"You?" They all asked in unison.

"Yeah, like you said, who would want to hurt the Congress-woman? I'm a fan. I can do it."

The captain smiled wryly, but looking straight at the two officers, now both at attention, he nodded his head and said, "Okay Garrison, the job is yours." The men backed out of the office, shutting the door as they left.

The captain turned his full attention on me. "Don't fuck this up." With that, he sat down behind his obsessively clean desk, dialed the telephone and started to talk. I stood for a minute or so, waiting for more instructions. They didn't come. A wave of his hand dismissed me, and I left to get details for my assignment from his secretary.

Carole introducing Shirley Chisholm at the Women's History Project of the Akron Area, 1991. The congresswoman, who had already retired, took time to save my career for a second time by coming to Akron as our special guest. Her presence revitalized the project and gave it renewed significance. *The Carole J. Garrison Family Archive.*

Shirley Chisholm, 1991. *The Carole J. Garrison Family Archive.*

I had just convinced my boss to let me work the executive protection detail for Congresswoman Shirley Chisholm — an African American woman representing New York's 12th Congressional District — and the first woman to run for U.S. president. In those days, Atlanta's Hartsfield Airport had one gate and we could deplane VIPs right on the tarmac. What could go wrong?

A beautiful young woman dressed in traditional African clothes was waiting for me at the Mayor's office. She would represent city hall when I met the plane. At the airport, I checked in with the local police unit that covered Hartsfield.

"Garrison, that plane is late. Grab yourself some breakfast. It will be at least an hour," the duty sergeant assured me — smiling, and waving me off.

The coffee shop was crowded and noisy and soon all my attention was on the mayor's aid. Over the last of our coffee, she told me that greeting the Congresswoman was her very first assignment.

I checked my watch — plenty of time. The sergeant had said at least an hour. Better earlier than late, I decided and motioned the waitress over for the check. Within minutes my patrol car was parked on the tarmac at the Congresswoman's scheduled gate. No one was around. No iridescent green jackets and light sticks were anywhere to be seen. Finally, I found a baggage handler and asked why they weren't getting ready for the incoming flight from La Guardia.

"The plane with the Congresswoman?" he asked.

"Yeah, that one," I said, now suddenly sorry I had eaten so many pancakes.

"That plane was here and gone an hour ago."

The Mayor's aid went pale. "Don't worry," I said, trying, and failing, to reassure either of us. "She's a smart woman; I'm sure she made her way to the hotel.

"It's not the Congresswoman I'm worried about," she replied, her eyes downcast and frowning.

In those days everyone in town had a police scanner and every call went over the same channel. The entire department and city could hear every transmission. I called in.

"Officer Garrison, I've lost Shirley Chisholm."

"Garrison, drive your vehicle north on I-75 to the Tennessee border. Turn the car into the highway patrol. They'll return it to us."

I DROPPED THE MAYOR'S AID off at the hotel where the Congresswoman was speaking and drove back to HQ. I marched silently through a gauntlet of laughing and cat-calling to my captain's office. His secretary was smiling. The women staff always smiled when a policewoman was in trouble. They didn't like us being there.

"He's waiting for you," she said, her fingers patting her smiling lips making her amusement all that obvious.

I walked in, closing the door behind me. I stood awkwardly and silently in front of his desk, noting the details of his office as if I was cataloging his belongings for an inventory. He sat back in his leather chair, rocking slightly. He didn't exactly glare at me standing in front of his desk, but he wasn't smiling either. Finally, he clapped his stocky hands together, drummed his short, plump fingers on his neat, almost bare—with the exception of a Tiffany pen set and his prized Double Midnight Jelly Peach blown glass paper-weight from Maui—gleaming walnut desk. Then he looked across at me and laughed. I stopped cataloging.

"It's not funny. I have two children to support." There was no way I'd snitch on anyone.

"Don't worry. The Police Commissioner called. We're not to take any action against you. The Mayor wants you to pick up Representative Chisholm and return her to the airport for her flight back to New York. Dismissed."

I CHECKED THE AIR IN MY TIRES and hoped there was no sugar in my gas tank. I pulled up in front of the hotel just in time to see the Mayor's aid, her lovely dark skin glowing, walking down the steps with a thin, distinguished looking black woman in a navy blue power suit. The Congresswoman sat in front passenger seat. "I don't like doors that don't open from the inside," she said, her smile getting wider as she laughed at her own joke, and maybe a hint of a past youthful indiscretion. My pulse, which by then had reached tachycardia levels, returned to normal.

We drove out of the downtown area, maneuvered onto the I85 south-bound ramp and headed back to the airport.

"Congresswoman Chisholm, I understand why you intervened on the mayor's aide's behalf. She was an innocent victim of a prank. But why did you bother to save my skinny white butt?" The words spilled out like water rushing over a broken dam. I had to ask, I had to know.

"Honey," she said, smiling and patting my knee. "We gals got to stick together."

SHIRLEY CHISHOLM'S CONSTANT SMILE was the result of a malocclusion, but the generosity of spirit it signaled was the result of her character. The story was a favorite of mine to share. Some twenty years later, I needed a star to resurrect interest in our eleventh annual women's history celebration in Akron, Ohio, an event whose luster and popularity was ebbing. No longer a cop, I was director of women's studies at the university and organizer of the annual program. It was our signature event.

"I don't know if she'll remember me. It happened years ago," I protested

"Try, Carole, try. Think what a coup it would be to get her here — what it would mean to increase the celebration's diversity and community outreach." The planning committee hammered away at the idea until I agreed to call her. She answered her own phone, and I heard her smile through the telephone wire connecting me to New York City.

"Why yes, I remember you," she said after I recounted our meeting.

"I have a favor to ask. You once saved my job, and I'm asking you to do it again."

Within minutes she had agreed and I ended the conversation with a few details and a promise to send her the itinerary and travel arrangements.

"I don't know how to thank you for agreeing to do this. It means everything to me and to the event."

"Oh, honey," she said, "We gals got to stick together." I'm positive she was smiling when she said it.◆

CHAPTER 4

Where's the Sugar?

MOM, YOU PROMISED YOU'D GET sugar for my cereal. I'm not eating." The argument that followed had almost caused my daughter to miss her school bus and made me late to work. Sugar prices had skyrocketed with the Cuban embargo, and I had been reduced to occasionally pinching sugar packets from the local deli when I stopped for a cup of caffeine on my way to the precinct.

The waitresses had stared at me the first few times, but I just hitched up my gun belt and pretended not to notice their disapproving looks. However, I had run out of packets so, to prevent another fight the next day, I had to repeat my larceny. At least I was in civilian clothes, but I still felt cheap stuffing handfuls of sugar packets into my purse.

His bulk filled up the open doorway to my office, blocking the light from the industrial-size fluorescent hall lights. He seemed amused as he listened to me rattling off the daily crime report to the WAXZ reporter on the other end of the phone. After finally convincing the reporter that I wasn't holding anything back and that, no, I wasn't interested in sharing an afternoon delight, I hung up and turned to face Lt. Loumaikis.

I smiled up at my friend. Terry worked vice and occasionally got me sprung from my current office work on legislation and public relations to do what he considered "real police work."

"What 'ya need? Got a female perp on her period?" I asked. I hoped not. The squad often called me when a body cavity search was required on a female they suspected of being "on the rag." Otherwise, the guys were perfectly happy to search away. I had already been having a bad day, and it wasn't even lunch time yet.

"Naw, nothing like that. I came to warn you," Terry said.

"Warn me?" My eyes narrowed, and I felt a little shiver of concern. I was often the focus of unwanted attention, pranks and threats—both subtle and obvious. The Atlanta Police Department in the mid-seventies was not always a nice place to work, especially for a divorced mother.

"Yeah, Cap is rampaging through headquarters doing surprise gun inspections." Terry smirked as he said it.

"What floor is he on?"

"Third, working his way down here."

"Damn, where is that thing?" I swore. I was in civilian clothes and my gun, if I had remembered to bring it, should be in my handbag.

Terry walked over to a side chair, bent down, grabbed something and stood, holding out my purse. My Smith & Wesson .38 regular wasn't in it but my smaller snub nose was. So my only worry was whether I'd remembered to load it during all that fuss about eating Cheerios from the discount store. I had started to reach down into the bag when Captain Miller's balding head peered around the door frame. "Knock, knock. Hi, Lieutenant. Got some place you need to be; maybe clear the mob?" he asked Terry. "Weapons inspection, officer," he said to me.

"Yes, sir," Terry replied, backing out of the door into a small crowd of policemen who had gathered outside my office. As he pulled the door closed behind him, I heard him telling them to get the hell out of the hall and find some work to do. Scuffling and a few muffled hoots were followed by silence. I looked at the captain and he nodded. "No need to entertain the troops today. Just get out your weapon."

My purse lay open on my desk. Captain Miller looked from it to me. I smiled. He smiled and looked back at the purse. I inhaled, stuck my hand into the bag and pulled out my smaller weapon—the one I carried in my purse when I wore civilian clothes and in an ankle holster while in uniform. Even as I opened the cylinder, before handing the gun over to the captain, sugar began to pour from the barrel.

"I can explain," I said.

"Please don't."

"But . . ."

"No 'buts,' Garrison. Clean the damn gun and report to my office at 1300 hours."

Captain Miller opened the door and stepped into the apparently vacant hallway. I sighed with frustration at myself as well as relief at the unexpected delay in receiving a reprimand. Terry came back into the office mere seconds later, growling something under his breath, and shut the door again.

"No bullets?" he asked.

I shook my head and looked down at the small hill of sugar on my desk. "Didn't come up . . ." I flapped a hand at the white pile and continued, "I have to clean my weapon and report to Miller's office at 1300."

"No can do. We need you. We're doing a raid and need an undercover female cop to get us in. You're a female, and you just happen to be in civvies. I'll call my boss and get him to square it with Miller. Let's go."

In Atlanta in the 1970s, when a suspect was killed while committing a crime, the SWAT team celebrated a reduction in the crime rate. Black officers were not allowed to change in the headquarters' locker room; they dressed at the Butler Street YMCA. When a female needed to be searched, I was called. When my daughters needed me at home, I was always working a double shift.

So when I had finished my master's degree at night school, I realized that my calling was not to search women's private parts or to nick sugar. What's that old adage? "Those who can, do; those who can't, teach." I was going to teach—impart to those who were doing the job how to do it better. A dead suspect was not crime reduction. I left the Atlanta PD, went on to get a PhD and have since taught applied ethics in policing until this very day.♦

CAMBODIAN JOURNAL: PART TWO

Preface

Unable to readjust to normal life after my year of living dangerously, I sought a way to return to Cambodia — the place I most connected with living life by the day. My opportunity came in 1995 when I was hired as the executive director of the CCC, The Committee for Cooperation in Cambodia. ■

CHAPTER 1

Journal Entry: The Fire
Phnom Penh, Cambodia, 1996

"Nobody likes the Vietnamese, only Hun Sen does."

—Anonymous

I HAD ARRIVED IN EARLY 1996 to take up my position as the executive director of the Committee for Cooperation in Cambodia, CCC, a network of international and local non-governmental organizations, NGOs. Phnom Penh had only recovered slightly since the civil war and the Khmer Rouge had devastated the country, pushing modernization back decades in the capital city and perhaps centuries in the countryside. The city was bustling with reconstruction and development as well as hordes of foreign investors, expatriates and peasants all looking for opportunity. The international community was pouring aid and grants into both the government and the NGO community. Corruption and decadence flourished like invasive weeds gone amuck.

My small street was a metaphor for the glaring cultural and economic gaps in Phnom Penh at that time. Mansions and squatter shacks stood in stark contrast to each other within the same space. I lived in a small two-story house, with a warm brown hardwood structure upstairs and a cement block bottom. The house had one bedroom, a tiny dining area and an even smaller kitchen where I cooked mango chicken and mango pancakes when my Cambodian friends brought me bushels of ripe mangos — my favorite fruit. The house may have been cramped, but it had a western toilet and an indoor bathtub. What more could I want?

Like most single dwellings, the house sat within a walled compound with ten-foot-high walls topped with glass shards. The front yard, instead of the typical lush garden of banana trees, orchids and a riot of colorful bougainvillea, was a cement courtyard about thirty-five feet wide by forty feet long. A single loganberry tree shaded the small front porch, providing shade during the heat of the day and a resting place for local bats at night. The stone bottom part of the house — which I must admit I had never entered — opened onto the cement courtyard. The big iron gates at the end of it fronted a narrow dirt lane. I lived directly across from a vast compound surrounding an abandoned Buddhist pagoda that hosted a squatters' village of unthinkable density. Cambodians identified many of these squatter settlements, which had sprung up around Phnom Penh since the early 1990s, as Vietnamese areas, despite knowing that Cambodians lived in them as well.

Leaving in the morning to go to work, I often crossed paths with Vietnamese taxi girls on the way home from their evening's labors, still wearing heavy makeup and gaudy slinky dresses, to sleep the day away in dingy huts with no electricity or water. In the evenings, the children and adults who inhabited a warren of small rooms carved into the stone wall encircling the pagoda shyly exchanged smiles and waves as I returned home to my new neighborhood.

We had no shared language, only little gestures of friendship and trust. Soon a familiar pattern emerged. The children ran out into the lane when they heard my car or the creaking of my gates being opened.

Cameras were a rare commodity among the local people, one of the most obvious victories for the anti-tech reign of terror by the Khmer Rouge. Very few even had access to important event pictures such as wedding portraits, much less family photos. The cost of processing a roll of film was equivalent to a week's pay for the average family. Like me, most expatriates working in Cambodia were on a holiday from their western, modern, high-tech lives but, like all good tourists, we brought cameras and video equipment. I began to routinely take snapshots of children, families and eventually special occasions when my neighbors finally got up the nerve to ask. Then I would get the film developed and hand out the eagerly awaited photos.

Soon my new friends were waving to me, shouting my name or occasionally bringing me some unnamed and often unrecognizable Vietnamese delicacy. They waited patiently for me in the evenings, but when they saw me crossing the lane with an envelope in my hand, all the shyness gave way to giggles, smiles and the slightest of bows of the elders' heads.

NOT EVERYONE WAS AS pleased to have Vietnamese neighbors as I was. As I read the op-eds in the *Cambodian Daily* and heard the political posturing on the news, I could imagine a meeting of the prime minister with his cabinet. My neighbors were squatters. My neighbors were illegal immigrants.

"All the illegal Vietnamese immigrants in the city must be cleaned out," Sophara, deputy governor of Phnom Penh, enjoined his associates. Heads nodded solemnly around the room before turning from him to their leader, Hun Sen. "Yuon are not allowed to live in the land of Khmer... Yuon must go and live in Yuon land," he said with his hands pressed together as if in prayer, his fingertips brushing against his cruel smile. He stood, bowed slightly to the men and women sitting

Carole and Vietnamese house guests sharing a communal dinner on the cement floor of her gated compound after the pagoda fire, Phnom Penh, 1996. *The Carole J. Garrison Family Archive.*

Carole and Vietnamese house guests at the farewell dinner, Phnom Penh, 1996. It was then they wished me to live a hundred years. *The Carole J. Garrison Family Archive.*

Robin opened a free medical clinic at Carole's house for victims of the pagoda fire, 1996. *The Carole J. Garrison Family Archive.*

around the large gleaming teak conference table and, together with his two fierce female body guards, left the room.

Only Chea Sophon, the finance minister, offered any resistance to the idea that the Vietnamese should be removed. "We should remember that our 'guests' are considered good and reliable workers, much better than Khmer. Many builders exclusively use Vietnamese workers in the construction business. Maybe... we can shift them outside the city."

A few cabinet members snickered. Chea Sophon was heavily into construction and making millions of dollars off of government contracts. Besides, the leader had left before the finance minister had said anything. Unpatriotic, they thought.

The minister of the interior, Chea Sim, rose from his chair, with his hand covering most of his mouth, which made his soft voice even harder to hear. The others leaned in out of respect, as well as fear. He was a close confidant of the leader. "To sympathize with or to trust the Vietnamese at all is to forget the injustice of their taking Kampuchea Krom lands. The fact is, Yuon are Yuon. There are only those who are looking for the opportunity to take everything."

Chea Sophon, chafing from the earlier reaction of his colleagues, rose directly across from the interior minister to chastise him. "Cambodia's lack of adequate border controls has allowed Vietnamese to infiltrate Khmer lands illegally. I think that is your failure." As Sophara stood, both ministers retreated to their chairs. "I don't care where you put them, or how you get them out. Just put them

*outside of the capital." Satisfied that they had reached an
understanding, Sophara lit one of his imported Chinese
cigarettes, took a deep draw and waited for suggestions
on how to accomplish the leader's wishes.*

I HAD GONE HOME FOR LUNCH and a nap instead of taking
the noon siesta at my office. I smelled it before I heard it; I heard
the roar before I saw it. The ancient pagoda, hundreds of years
old, was going up like kindling, the flames shooting forty and fifty
feet into the air. Black smoke was pouring across the road, and
a huge burst of flame gave off so much heat that I could feel it
on my porch. I could see huge billows of black smoke spewing
from the interior of the squatter camp. Shouting people were
rushing everywhere, carrying babies, meager possessions, prized
TVs and boom boxes. The flames climbed higher, but the wind
was blowing in the opposite direction from my house. Khmer
friends came over to make sure I was okay, turned off my stove
and electricity and begged me to close my gates.

"Shut your gates, mum," they shouted. "Please," they begged,
"Close the gates before all the Vietnamese squatters run in here.
Any Vietnamese who seem kind-hearted may easily *trewlop
dae,* change face."

"No," I yelled from my porch. "Open the gates wide and
tell the people living in the wall to bring their belongings and
children inside."

They came. They came with sewing machines and bedding;
they came with toddlers and infants. They came until there was
no room left in my small compound and the gates had to be
closed and locked.

We all stood watching as the entire shanty town of two
to three hundred shacks became a wall of fire, an inferno of
immense heat. Most of the expatriates on the street fled in their
cars, locking their gates behind them, but the three of us who
lived closest to the pagoda stayed and kept our houses open.

My yard looked like a flea market, quickly taking on the appearance of a refugee camp. I bandaged toes, held little Vietnamese children who were trembling and reeking of ash and fear, and sedated one of the old ladies. I offered whatever moral support I could to those families who had lived across from me. Miraculously, there had been only one reported death.

That night six or seven youngsters, terrified from their ordeal, came upstairs to the safety of my house to sleep in my bedroom with me. They smelled like gerbils, only more sooty and dirty. Outside, little pink and blue mosquito net tents sprang up like mushrooms across the courtyard. The old women and babies slept in the downstairs salon, or what was left of it. When I opened the doors to the bottom stone part of the house, many adults stowed inside the few belongings they had managed to save, including motorbikes and sewing machines. I gave the key to one man who spoke a little English. Others slept in the yard while most of the men stayed outside the gates and guarded what was left of their homes.

"SHE CAN'T DO IT. It isn't in her brief!" loudly complained an older, portly woman. Several people were gathered around a large teak wood table, all eyes on the speaker. The meeting room was small for the size of the table; the walls were covered with local art—canvas wall hangings of peasants planting and harvesting in the rice paddies—and there was a large stone bust of Jayavarman VII, the Angkor period king who had brought Buddhism to Cambodia.

The woman continued to complain. "I have been here since the mid-1970s, when she and all the rest of you were afraid to come to Cambodia. I have built trust between me and Hun Sen, and I'm not going to stand by and watch her destroy it."

The head of Cambodia's first think tank, Eva had a long history of activism, going all the way back to the American women's health collective in the 1960s. The legend was that Hun Sen was devoted to her because she had nursed the strongman back to life when he was injured during the Vietnam invasion to rid the country of Pol Pot. Eva and I took up a lot of oxygen...so, when we occupied the same space, it was difficult for anyone to breathe. We were natural rivals—I was an upstart in her mind—and this was a perfect opportunity for her to be rid of me.

"What do you suggest?" Henrik, the tall lean head of the Dutch NGO, Oxfam Novib, asked. "Do we stand by and do nothing?"

"Exactly. Nothing," Eva replied.

The woman from OXFAM UK, a small dark Indian, agreed. "If no NGOs follow her, she will lose her credibility as director and will have to step down. If they do follow her, we will have a harder time getting government cooperation. It will be bad for all of us in the long term, and for Cambodia as well."

Henrik added dryly, "Hun Sen wants to divest us of our tax-exempt status. We can't give him an excuse."

"Enough! We are all aware of the consequences of publicly confronting Hun Sen. Contact the other NGO directors, get them in line. I don't want anyone offering aid to the victims of the fire—no one." Eva turned a stony glare at the directors in the meeting room, which froze them all into compliance.

The Cambodian Red Cross, which was led by none other than Hun Sen's wife, had refused to help because so many of the victims were Vietnam squatters and the government was committed to removing them from the country. To make the situation even direr, the International Red Cross gave into political expediency, refusing to provide aid lest they run afoul of government disapproval.

"BEFORE, I ALWAYS THOUGHT that Khmer people were gentle and polite and didn't harm others because they are Buddhist," Tinh told me through my interpreter on the second night of the encampment in my courtyard. "I never thought Khmer people could be as cruel as this, to burn us out and to leave us to die," Tinh continued, pondering what she as well as many of her Vietnamese neighbors had held to be a peaceful coexistence with the country's Khmer ethnic majority.

Ho Thy Nam, who for ten years had lived in close proximity to Tinh as a fellow denizen of the squatters' community, was equally bewildered by the repugnance his Khmer neighbors had exhibited during the course of the fire and its aftermath. In broken English, he stated the more reasonable words of Cambodia's King Sihanouk regarding the relationship between Vietnam and Cambodia: "Heaven has made it our neighbor for eternity."

Neighbors don't treat neighbors this way, I thought.

"Why is it that Cambodian people despise Vietnamese people?" Tinh mused, as she and her anxious family worried about where they would live, and whether the Cambodian immigration police would come soon to repatriate them over the border into Vietnam.

I DIDN'T HAVE ENOUGH GRASP of their language to explain to Tinh's family the centuries-old enmity between these eternal neighbors and their relentless squabbling over borders and resources. I couldn't read them the recent spate of articles claiming that unidentified Vietnamese leaders were planning to overtake and incorporate numerous provinces of Cambodia—an unsupported claim that nevertheless was strongly held by Khmers, both in Cambodia and abroad. I couldn't account for the fact that, even in Phnom Penh, where land ownership is a complicated issue for Khmers themselves, Vietnamese have always been seen as trespassers, and despite many Cambodians living in the pagoda squatter settlement, it was considered a Vietnamese area.

IT WAS WINTER and, even in that tropical land, the night air was humid and cool. Inside the burned-out pagoda, families slept on the wet burnt earth; inside my compound, they slept on cold damp cement. People were cold; people were sick; and people were hungry. They needed help.

"I can't. I'm meant to be in Sihanukeville for the weekend. You'll have to find someone else," Robin responded.

Robin, the Australian embassy doctor, was a friend...sometimes even a lover...and, for the moment, my best hope of getting some medical help for the squatters. He tried to elevate his short stature by raising his shoulders, perhaps thinking that this gesture would convince me that I couldn't wheedle him into giving up his holiday at Cambodia's rustic and beautiful seaside resort on the Gulf of Thailand. It only made him look comical.

"Robin, you of all people can't turn your back on these people. They need you. If not you, who?" That plea always got to him. I loved it. "What's so important anyway? You can go to the beach next weekend."

His face reddened, and his eyes averted mine. "No, it must be this weekend," he insisted.

Puzzled, I stared at him for a long time. I couldn't imagine why a weekend at the beach could be so important. I knew that he didn't give a damn about the government—or even his own embassy's unwillingness to help the fire victims—so what could it be? I decided to up the ante. "If just one of those babies dies for lack of paracetamol, I shall never forgive you."

"I'll stay, but perhaps I won't ever forgive you."

We set up a clinic on my porch to treat infants and toddlers for exposure, colds and dehydration. The line of adults and children snaked over the dirt lane, across my cement courtyard and up the stairs to the small balcony. Robin handed out aspirin, took temperatures, gave reassuring advice and finally confessed to me that he had missed a secret rendezvous with a mystery woman because of me. I tried the old cliché, "If it's meant to be..." Although he grimaced, I knew that he would rather be in our little clinic than anywhere else. The Vietnamese who were now living in my compound helped to manage the long line of refugees and passed out blankets, tarps and mosquito nets that had been dropped off at my house by other NGOs who joined with me to violate the ban.

I might have been the executive director of the CCC, but I didn't have actual programs, resources or staff to provide rice and other necessities for survival. At the risk of losing my job, I was able to convince some of the less politically dependent NGOs, notably Lutheran World Service, to bring bags of rice to my compound as they wouldn't actually be distributing it—just storing it. Once the two-and-a-half tons of rice was delivered to my house, the Vietnamese men who lived inside my compound carried the hundred-pound sacks on their backs to the burned-out pagoda and passed the rice out to everyone, Khmer and Vietnamese alike—whoever needed or wanted it. They worked while much of Phnom Penh stood by indifferently and watched.

AS IT HAPPENED, I had already rented a larger house across town before the fire, so my guests and I had to leave my compound by week's end. The majority of people had drifted away from the burn site, finding new places to shelter, but all of my guests stayed with me until moving day. At night I would see their little cooking fires and smell the exotic Asian aromas as the smoke curled up towards my little porch. Several of the children now slept under a net tent on my porch. Except for helping at the free clinic, most days I left for my office, emotionally drained from fighting with the heads of the large NGOs who wanted to skewer me alive for aiding the refugees against government wishes, while my community went about the business of finding work and shelter.

ON THE EVENING BEFORE I was to move to my new house, I arrived home to a frenzy of activity. Food was cooking everywhere, the children were scrubbed and blankets were laid out neatly in a large circle. Using their own version of Pidgin English, my guests made it clear that they wanted me to join them for a last dinner together. Everyone had contributed to the community meal, which was a genuine feast. My security guard translated my guests' wish for me: that I live more than one hundred years. I sat cross-legged on the ground, surrounded by happy people eating *pho* and savory pancakes called *banh xeo,* while I fumbled with my chopsticks and tried to make conversation. But words did not matter; we were celebrating life.♦

CHAPTER 2

Journal Entry: Angel of Buddha
Cambodia, 1995-1997

THE ROOM WAS SMALL. Sun streamed in through the open window, overpowering the lazily rotating ceiling fan and framing the young woman talking to me in an aura of golden light. "Does it matter?" she asked.

"I'd prefer one of the girls. I've raised two of my own."

"Why don't you adopt Tevi?" Violy, the director of the small private orphanage replied. She was a petite woman, dark-skinned and neatly dressed in the traditional Cambodian way of school teachers—in a dark, long blue skirt and a pressed, tailored white cotton blouse.

"Tevi doesn't like me."

Violy shrugged. "Tevi doesn't like anyone."

I didn't answer. Instead, I looked around the tiny director's office of the Canada House orphanage in Phnom Penh, processing the fact that I was precariously close to adopting a six-year-old. Not just any six-year-old but, per her records, a girl whose given name means Angel of Buddha. This angel had already been adopted and returned to the Canada House since arriving at the orphanage a month before her mother's death five years earlier.

My head filled with random facts. Children who reached the age of seven in a non-government orphanage must be turned over to government services. This policy was supposed to protect older children from being adopted by pedophiles; the rationale was that no potential parent would want a child older than a newborn or a toddler who would come to see the adoptive household as his or her true family. But it was no secret that the government sold these children to brothels to satisfy the sex-tourism trade and to tycoons for use as domestic workers. The situation was especially dire for female children, as AIDS had been rampant since the United Nations' peace-keeping mission and young, healthy girls were at a premium in the brothels of Southeast Asia.

Still, I asked myself, "Why?" Why should I take on this responsibility at the age of fifty-six? Didn't my father used to say, "If you see trouble in the road, you must stop and help"? Or was that a 1960s Baby Boomer motto? Maybe I'd be better off following the advice of a book title that I once saw on a library shelf: *If You See the Buddha on the Road, Kill Him.* I even suspected that I was trying to make amends for a long-ago abortion. And, although I fervently hoped not, perhaps I was trying to impress my current love interest, who worked with the orphans and adored them. That shallow motivation would set a record low, even for me. In the end, I had to admit that I was in full throttle savior mode — attempting to write a happy ending for the craziest fairy tale of them all.

Rather than make an immediate decision, I thought about my whereabouts. The orphanage was founded by a Canadian woman who had worked in Southeast Asia since the Vietnam War — first in Vietnam, then in Cambodia. On a late afternoon in April 1975, she had stood in the bright sun outside the Tan

Son Nhut airfield near Saigon, with the twenty-some orphans she had taken off the overcrowded U.S. Air Force C-5A Galaxy transport plane, and watched as it went down shortly after take-off. Twenty years later she was still rescuing orphans. She had personally provided sanctuary for Tevi, taking her in along with seven of her eight older siblings. Only Tevi remained. The others had run away soon after their mother's death.

Violy looked at me expectantly, her smile barely camouflaging her impatience as she waited for me to decide. Impulsively, as if driven by an emotional obsession, I said, "Let's see if she will have me." Flabbergasted at hearing my own voice, I could only hope that Tevi's rejection might provide an escape route from the temporary madness that had overcome me.

For weeks, sullen and unrelenting, she refused my gifts by pushing most of them out through the big iron gates. When we were together at a group outing for the orphans, she would purposely find another lap to sit on. If I took her out alone to get some ice cream, she would watch it melt rather than eat it in front of me. Nevertheless, I had presented her with a small emerald ring that had not come back through the gate. In fact, Tevi was caught on camera pushing the ring into her little friend BoPah's face and telling her, "I have my own mommy now." (BoPah had been adopted by the family who had returned Tevi to the orphanage.)

YEARS LATER, WHEN MY MOTHER asked me if I had carefully considered the consequences of adopting a hyperactive six-year-old orphan who was eighty percent malnourished, I replied, "Mom, really. Had I thought about it, I would never have done it."

Mom's eyebrows arched a little higher on her forehead as I mentally played over the dozen or so years since Tevi had proclaimed she had a mother. I skipped the challenges of returning to America earlier than anticipated because of Cambodia's political coup. I ignored the fact that Tevi's starting grade school

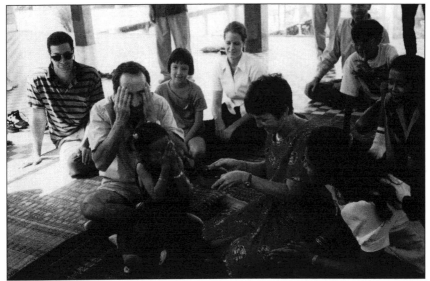

Carole, Robin and Tevi at her Cambodian adoption ceremony surrounded by expatriate friends and local staff who traveled from Phnom Penh to the Skon pagoda to celebrate the occasion, in Kâmpóng Cham, Cambodia, 1997. *The Carole J. Garrison Family Archive.*

Gert, Tevi, Lucky (Carole's staff driver) and another child from the orphanage on an afternoon outing. Gert had traveled alone from the U.S. to Phnom Penh to meet her future granddaughter. 1996. *The Carole J. Garrison Family Archive.*

with limited English made arithmetic word problems about snow skiing as difficult for her as thermo dynamics, and that her cognitive handicaps discovered in second grade meant that she couldn't process the *Henry and Mudge* reader. I only thought about the little girl who had disrupted and enhanced my life, giving it challenge and purpose. I considered how Tevi had rewired my family, encouraging my daughters to have children of their own, and how she taught me that the heart that loves more has more love to give.

Returning my attention to my mom, I smiled and said, "But aren't we glad I did?"♦

CHAPTER 3

Journal Entry: Not Goodbye
Phnom Penh, Cambodia, 1997

C NN SEEMED TO BE FILMING a horrific battle in another country. Excited reporters cautioned foreigners to remain indoors and not travel outside of the district home to most of Phnom Penh's Western expats. The coup had caused serious devastation had been caused by rockets launched in the direction of the airport and the main road out of the country toward Thailand, but most of the city and the rest of Cambodia had been spared. No spirals of black smoke hung in the air or bursts of gunfire could be seen or heard after the first early hours of Hun Sens' government takeover.

Virtual prisoners, we were confined to a cordoned-off section of the city. We could not leave our residences after dark or venture too far away from them even in the daylight. Our information came via international cable television, our cell phones and, occasionally, the Australian embassy's radio. We called business contacts in Bangkok, but no one was able to offer much hope or assistance.

Robin, the Australian embassy's doctor, began securing seats for people we knew on a medical evacuation flight that was leaving in two days for Bangkok. I was the executive director of CCC, a network of humanitarian organizations. I spent my time organizing the NGO sector's response to the coup. The imminent evacuation made us confident that the worst was over, so we ignored curfew and walked to the director of CARE's home for a small dinner party.

The ring of my cell phone shattered the façade of normalcy that the dinner was intended to celebrate. The urgency in the caller's voice was enough to terrify me, even before details could be obtained from his nervous, choppy English. "Hun, Hun hurt. Hun needs Dr. Robin. Hun come to hospital. Hun hurt, come now." Hun, a Khmer friend, had been injured, but it was impossible to understand the severity or cause of her plight.

I looked blankly at the small phone in my hand and felt my stomach lurch, "Where are you? What is happening? I don't understand," I cried into the receiver.

I rose from my chair, as Robin stared curiously at me.

"Who's that?" "What's going on?"

"I think it's someone calling about Hun. I think she's hurt and at Calmette Hospital. We need to go. We need to go now," I said, moving toward the door.

"Are you crazy? There's a curfew. Armed soldiers are prowling the streets. You can't go. I am not taking you," Robin said sternly, while the others all nodded in agreement.

Numbly, I sat back down. Helpless to do anything, I tried to make sense out of the call and that moment, which had brought the war on CNN into my life. Why would Hun be hurt? Why would she be in Calmette Hospital? Why couldn't I get there? Hun lived somewhere out toward the airport. I imagined that she had been injured as she tried to reach home from the small market near the waterfront, where she exchanged money and sold her husband's jewelry. More questions roiled around in my head. How badly was she hurt? Who was taking care of her? Where were her husband and baby Mey-Mey? There were no answers and less options. No matter how pleadingly I looked at Robin, he did not move from his spot but stayed rooted to his chair!

"Carole, relax. We can't go tonight. I'll take you in the ambulance tomorrow, first thing in the morning." Then, as if I were a child begging for some promised treat, he said, "I promise, first thing."

I STAYED AWAKE ALL THAT NIGHT worrying about Hun—sweet, gentle Hun, whose young life had already known more than its share of hardship and tragedy. I had met Hun my first time in Cambodia during the UN peacekeeping mission. She was a moneychanger in the old central market, Psaa Thmey, in the heart of Phnom Penh. She spoke English, French and German—probably a little Russian, too. She was a natural-born salesperson. I'm not sure why we connected—most likely due to her ability to speak English—but we danced and jockeyed, bantered and withdrew, and finally bonded. She captivated me with her shocking tales of life in a children's labor camp during the Pol Pot period, hiding in the forest at night to avoid being molested by the male guards. Hun had bad acne, and I procured her a supply of antibiotics that the UN passed out to UN workers as prophylactics for infections. I was happy to give her my whole supply, as they dried out my vaginal fluids and made me susceptible to all kinds of itchy stuff that men didn't suffer. But it worked on her acne and, soon after her skin cleared, she met her true love—a young jewelry maker. I was invited to their wedding the following spring. I gave Hun one hundred dollars, US, her monthly earnings, as my gift. When I returned to her mother's house for dinner a few weeks later, there was an outsized wardrobe made of local hardwood with GARRISON carved across the lintel.

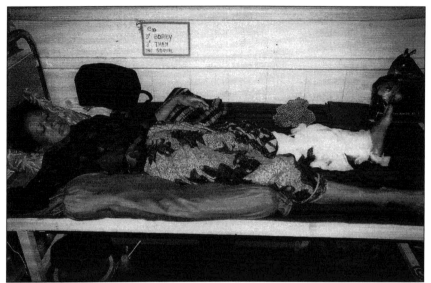

On July 5, 1997, the 2nd Prime Minister led a coup overthrowing the government and taking power. My friend Hun laid in a hospital bed with shrapnel in her neck and legs. I made daily runs to bring her morphine and she would tell me that "I was her luck in Cambodia." Phnom Penh. *The Carole J. Garrison Family Archive.*

The political coup – Phnom Penh, Cambodia 1997. *The Carole J. Garrison Family Archive.*

Hun, Mey-Mey and Gert, and Hun's husband Kong while Gert was visiting Phnom Penh in 1996. *The Carole J. Garrison Family Archive.*

Carole and Hun in better times, Phnom Penh Cambodia, 1993. *The Carole J. Garrison Family Archive.*

I HAD RETURNED HOME TO THE U.S. after the successful elections in Cambodia. While there, I had found the authentic me, not just glimpsed it, but had also lived it—eyes wide open—gloriously, dangerously I had put myself in control. Sadly, not unlike a junkie falling off the wagon, the authentic me began to unravel as I fell easily back into the very same habit-driven lifestyle I had tried to escape by joining the UN mission. I missed the highs. I was still broken. It was an easy decision to take the offer to become the Executive Director of the CCC, Cambodian Committee for Cooperation—a network of all the humanitarian organizations operating in the country. So in 1995, just two years after returning home, I again boarded the huge jetliner for the 22 hour flight to Phnom Penh. I had unfinished business in Cambodia. I was going to assist in the country's recovery. I was going to complete my own recovery.

While I was back in the States, Hun had a son, who died shortly after birth of cerebral encephalitis. She was devastated. But when I returned to Cambodia two years later, Hun was pregnant with her second child. Mai-Mai, a plump healthy daughter, was born a few months later. Hun often brought the baby to my house to bathe her in the Western bathtub and cool her down from Cambodia's relentless heat. We borrowed each other's money. She shopped for me in the markets to keep me from being cheated because, as she put it, "Your face makes Cambodian people greedy." We took day trips to the lake; her mother made my favorite duck dish, and her sisters pampered me. Hun claimed that I was her luck in Cambodia. She had a healthy baby girl, a thriving business and a husband she adored. Her life was good.

IT WAS DAYS BEFORE WE COULD finally travel beyond the few blocks surrounding either my house or Robin's clinic. I drove warily to my office and began holding hectic rounds of meetings with non-government organizations and embassies, trying to assess the situation. I put on-going projects in one place, to be easily found by the next director of the CCC. I took my staff's pensions out of the national bank and gave the cash to them in case the government failed. In the evenings, I helped Robin to arrange the airport evacuations. By bedtime I was exhausted. I had helped run the elections three years prior that this coup had just dismantled. I was angry, frustrated with the lack of international response and wanted to flee to the U.S., to my home, like those I helped evacuate each day.

On the fourth day following the coup, Robin drove me to Calmette Hospital — past obvious signs of heavy fighting, past soldiers in the streets with AKs, rockets and grenades, and past unseen but ever-present dangers. The walls of the waiting area were a dull yellowish-green, and the light came from naked bulbs that hung on skinny wires from the ceiling and gave everything a ghoulish pallor. I noticed a young woman — seriously injured, with many slashes to her back and cuts deep enough to possibly have punctured her lungs — lying on her stomach on a hard table, her soiled kramaa covering large, open cuts on her lower and middle back. A boy of about twelve, who was also seriously hurt, sat in a chair trying to be stoic. His injuries were ugly big holes and torn flesh. The boy's right arm was pressed tightly against his side. Dried blood covered his knuckles, wrists and ankles. Bruises had already appeared on his arms and neck. I had seen gunshot wounds when I was a cop, but I had never seen such carnage. My stomach heaved from the smell of blood, and my face felt numb, frozen in shock.

In a crowded hall just outside the waiting area I found Hun lying on a gurney, her eyes closed and motionless. Stunned, I took her hand in mine. A French woman in a nurse's uniform was the only medical person in sight. She explained that Hun had shrapnel lodged in her neck, the remnants of a rocket that had hit her house. However, all of the doctors had fled, and the hospital had no medical supplies.

Robin gave the nurse suggestions to ease Hun's pain and then taking the nurse aside, spoke to her privately. I saw her slip a vial of medicine, likely morphine, into her pocket and nod to Robin in agreement. Helpless to do more, I squeezed her hand and whispered her name. I felt the weakest pressure, but Hun's eyes were open and she was squeezing my hand back.

"You are my luck in Cambodia. Don't leave me," Hun begged from her make-shift hospital bed.

Robin had got me a seat on the morning's Australian transport to Penang Malaysia, and from there I had tickets home. My decision to return to the states from Cambodia was based less on fear than on my disenchantment with my job and disassociation with my sense of mission. Disillusioned with the expatriate community that was supposed to be the humanitarians of the world, my anger welled up, fueled by fear and fatigue; the dynamics of desperate people. I was confident that leaving was the right thing to do.

I WENT TO THE HOSPITAL and sat by Hun's bedside for a long while. I cupped her hand in mine; I wiped her brow; we made small talk. *"Oun sra-lun bong na,* I love you, too. I'll be back to visit soon, you'll see. Be brave." Whether because of the morphine or her love for me, she accepted my lies and smiled. I never saw her again.

Postscript: Hun was murdered during a robbery in front of her shop in the old market within weeks of her time at the hospital.◆

CHAPTER 4

Journal Entry: A Capital Offense
Penang, Malesia, 1997

> "Hun Sen has been accused of dictatorship and caus-
> ing riots in Cambodia after he staged a so-called coup
> d'état last week, ousting his co-premier, Prince Norodom
> Ranariddh."
>
> —*The Nation,* Bangkok, Friday, July 12, 1997

CAMBODIAN VILLAGERS REPEAT WORDS for emphasis, so when I say the rats were big-big, I mean they were huge vermin with glistening, pointed teeth and fiery red eyes. With a noise that cut like a sharp blade skimming down my spine, their nails scratched at the cement floor. They were emerging from dark corners to search for food, quite capable of tearing at human flesh. They ran up and down the hall, jumping over the low rail and scurrying across the sleeping women. Every few minutes one would leap up onto the platform where, horrified, I cradled Tevi in my arms and sat bolt upright, unable to sleep, unable to breathe, unable to hope.

I watched, amazed, as my newly adopted six-year-old daughter, Tevi, slept. Her lack of distress over the madness surrounding our last few days contrasted starkly with the terrified look in her eyes on the day that I first took her on an outing from Cambodian House. Tevi's naughty, bold exterior had melted away to reveal a small, frightened child with flapping elbows, knees, and darting eyes as we passed through the front gates of the orphanage and headed up the dirt road towards the wider world of Phnom Penh.

Not so on this morning, mere months later. As the dawn finally started to illuminate the cell where Tevi, the other inmates, the rats and I had spent the night, she woke and smiled at the two young Muslim women preparing for morning prayers. A young Indonesian woman waved at Tevi and spoke a few words in English. She waved back, hopped down from my lap and joined her. Tevi's survival skills had clicked in. In that moment, she knew that this woman was of more use to her than I was.

Breakfast arrived in the form of small loaves of white bread and a tin cup filled with water. My stomach ached for freedom, understanding and control—not food. I offered my portion to the young Indonesian woman, who took it gratefully. She shared the food and water with Tevi and began to occupy her with activity. As they played, she caught my eye, cuddled Tevi and smiled. Exhaling a flood of air, I slumped down on the cement and, drained from exhaustion, fell into a fitful sleep riddled with memories and waking dreams.

I had returned home to the United States after serving as a UN volunteer for the successful elections in Cambodia. While there, I had found the authentic me—not just glimpsed it, but also lived it—with eyes wide open. Gloriously, dangerously, I had put myself in control. But sadly, not unlike a junkie falling off the wagon, my authentic self began to unravel as I easily fell back into the very same habit-driven lifestyle I had tried to escape by joining the UN mission.

I missed the highs. I was still broken. So it was a simple decision to accept the offer to become the Executive Director of the Cambodian Committee for Cooperation — a network of all of the humanitarian organizations operating in the country. In 1995, just two years after returning home to Akron, Ohio, I again boarded a huge jetliner for the twenty-two-hour flight to Phnom Penh. I had unfinished business in Cambodia. I was going to assist in the country's recovery; I was going to complete my own recovery.

But Cambodia, barely emerged from decades of civil war and genocide, was reeling from the violence and uncertainty in the aftermath of the coup barely two and a half years into my return and six months after I had adopted Tevi. Armed men, some drunk and others angry at the coup's outcome, roamed the streets; health care professionals, who had abandoned the hospitals and neighborhoods where diplomats and expatriates lived, were in lock-down.

In my dreams, I saw my best friend Hun's face in pain from injuries sustained during the fighting, heard her beg me not to leave her.

More than anything else, it was my utter frustration with Cambodia's failed attempt at democracy that convinced me to take Tevi out of the country on an Australian military transport plane. In my altered state, I saw myself toss the small semi-automatic pistol into my purse. I had intended to protect us from dangers on the road to the airport. I had planned to leave the pistol with an embassy staff member before boarding the plane to Penang, Malaysia — the first stop on our way home to the States. But in the utter chaos at the airport, the gun remained my purse.

The stench of lunch drew me away from my memories. Guards brought in bundles of brown, paper-wrapped dried fish and rice. The other women eagerly grabbed their food, opened their portions and began eating with their hands. The smell overcame me, causing my body to fully shut down. I gave my unopened package of food to an elderly woman. Tevi sat close to her new friend and ate with considerable zest, using her hands as if it were her normal behavior. I sat in awe of her survival skills, honed beyond those of any Westerner. I had tried to make allies of our captors in the same calculating fashion as she made allies of the women who seemed most capable of enduring this place. While Tevi ate and played, I continued to review—this time wide awake—the events that had landed us in this hundred-year-old, rat-infested women's prison in Malaysia rather than on a jetliner winging our way to safety.

HAVING JUST FLED A WAR, getting stopped by a security official at the Penang airport on our way to Kuala Lumpur was a minor inconvenience. I had forgotten about the gun in my luggage until an officer asked me if I had something metal in my bag. I responded immediately by searching through my packed clothing, mentally identifying each piece by its texture as I groped for anything metal. Luckily, I had removed the magazine, so the gun was unloaded when I finally produced it.

"Madame, you will please come with me," the guard said politely. He marched Tevi and me away from the security area while the other travelers stared and whispered nervously, trying to guess my fate.

I was ushered into a small waiting room tainted by the heavy smell of stale cigarettes, where I convinced myself that, after explaining that the gun was unloaded and I meant no harm, the police would scold me, confiscate the weapon and send us on our way. A young police officer with a stern, almost scornful, face came into the room. "It is a holiday and my superiors are away," he said. "There is no one here but me." After a brief pause, he added, "This is very, very serious. You have broken the law, committed a capital crime, in my country." There was not the slightest hint of irony or bluff in his voice or manner.

A flood of explanations flowed from me in no order. "I'm sorry. I forgot that I even had that gun in my bag. It wasn't loaded; just take it and let us go. I must get to Kuala Lumpur to meet my brother. We should go now. I have this child with me. She is an orphan from Cambodia. We were evacuated. Drunken soldiers roamed the streets." The officer was unsympathetic. "You have committed a hanging offense; you can be hanged," he said. He left, and I sat.

People, I couldn't identify as officials or civilians, came in and out of the waiting room to look at the "American criminal." I played with Tevi and forced my mind to go blank. I had to control my imagination so as not to feed my fear. The time to catch the plane to Kuala Lumpur, Malaysia's capital and largest city, had come and gone. Occasionally, I was asked a few questions, notes were taken, and then I was abandoned again. I talked to everyone who wanted to talk, slowly leaking personal information in the hope that it would either serve to intimidate or to create an alliance.

Finally, a face with a different type of countenance, emitting both authority and kindness, entered the room. The assistant to The Chief gently spoke perfect English through perfect teeth. Tevi immediately sensed the promise of this visitor. She climbed in his lap and made him her newest friend. He looked and talked like a professional; he was moderate in his approach and clearly was not looking to create an untenable situation. I had to take a gamble and hope that this considerate official would be my ticket home.

We left the airport and went to the police station. I had already pulled out my folder of documents—adoption papers, résumé, passport—anything that would make me appear legitimate, worthy of sympathy and less suspicious or threatening. I had to match The Chief's professionalism and create a bridge for us to meet upon half-way.

I could feel a bond emerging but, when I was ordered to go into the back room for a mug shot as Tevi looked on with a mix of curiosity and apprehension, I knew my ordeal was far from over. I explained that I needed to contact my brother, Nat, who was expecting me in Kuala Lumpur that evening. Before I made the call, I asked the detective if I should tell Nat what was happening. "No," The Chief cautioned. "We believe you and want to find a way out of this. It will not help to bring in others."

I had to make a critical decision. If I followed his advice, I could fall into an abyss of obscurity, with weeks passing before anyone could ascertain my fate; however, if I ignored it and informed Nat of my situation, I risked severing the only bond I had managed to foster.

After much deliberation, I told my brother, "I can't get a flight to Kuala Lumpur for several days, so Tevi and I are going to hang out on the beach and relax. Don't worry, go on without me. I'll call you in the States when I know my itinerary."

Apologizing profusely, The Chief took Tevi and me to the women's jail in Penang, where I surrendered ten thousand dollars and our lives into the jailers' keeping.

HOURS PASSED AS I SAT WITH MY KNEES drawn up to my chin and my back pushed straight up against the wall. I tried to shut the odors out of my senses and quiet the rising turmoil that swelled in my chest, "Not another night; not another night here with the rats that circled around us with the intimacy of family pets," I whispered to myself. Uncertainty gave way to a fierce terror that seeped through to my consciousness. I was losing my strength to hysteria and could already see myself screaming at the cell bars, "I am an American! Let me out!"

Just then, at the very moment when I was dissolving into

a mass of panic-fueled fear, guards came to the cell door and motioned us out. The Chief smiled and said, "Let's go." As we hurried down the hall, away from the cell, he added "It's not over yet. I'm sorry I couldn't come earlier." I knew that Tevi and I were closer to getting home, but I couldn't determine how much closer. Despite The Chief's friendliness, there was still an atmosphere of caution.

We were taken to a clean, modern Muslim hotel. I was beyond exhaustion—functioning like a zombie robot. Every bit of my energy was focused on maintaining The Chief's support and making Tevi and me his top priority. Given my body's limited resources, eating, sleeping or even thinking beyond this immediate imperative could not be accomplished. Colors had disappeared and my world turned into a shadowy hell of black and white.

A thin-boned, older woman, who spoke little English and seemed quite uncomfortable with her responsibilities, supervised our house arrest. Our inability to communicate made our movements awkward. I didn't want to scare or alarm her, but the rules of our confinement were unclear. At first, even the bathroom was not considered a sanctuary worthy of privacy. A small respite from the tension came with her evening replacement—a jovial, younger woman who didn't appreciate being confined any more than we did.

Days passed and The Chief came and went, always stating as he left, "It's not sure yet." Then, one afternoon, his superior, the Police Commissioner, came to our hotel room. Surprisingly, he apologized for our night in jail, for keeping us under house arrest and for adding to our troubles after we had barely escaped the coup's aftermath. Although he told me that he understood why I had the gun, my hopes of emancipation were soon quashed by his departing words: "Working on it...shouldn't be long now." Another night, another endless day. More uncertainty, more delay. I had not talked to anyone who wasn't bound to me through incarceration since my call to Nat—a week earlier. Did anyone miss me yet?

The Chief arrived the following morning with mixed news. Government officials wanted me gone to avoid a potential international incident. They would confiscate the gun. "Of course," I heard myself saying. However, I was to fly to Kuala Lumpur and remain there under house arrest until I could catch a flight to the United States—a dicey scenario at best. Would the locals be sympathetic or hostile? How long would I be under house arrest? What would happen to Tevi? Each minute that passed increased the risk of my making a mistake, of having everything unravel.

"Could I fly to Singapore and go home from there?" I asked, trying to keep the desperation out of my voice. The Chief liked this suggestion. If it could be arranged, he and his officers would be free of me. It was also a tenuous situation for them, well outside the boundaries of their authority and expertise. Nothing was guaranteed. We all needed closure. Before The Chief took off yet again, he called the young, stern officer at the airport and told him to check out this possibility.

The Chief returned in the afternoon along with his lieutenant, a thin, middle-aged officer introduced to me as Lt. Teng. They were going to take Tevi and me sightseeing and shopping. Although I feigned appreciation, I was deflated to learn that their purpose was not to drive us to the airport.

The itinerary did not include the usual touristic tour locations. After a quick stop to admire a modern shopping center, we paid a visit to some snake handlers. The Chief held Tevi while I, in a show of bravado—or more likely mental and physical exhaustion—posed for photos holding a bloated, nine-foot boa on my arms.

Teng wanted me to pray and give thanks at the famous local Buddhist temple. He had noticed I wore a wooden Buddha on a chain around my neck. In their experience, Americans were Christians and I hadn't admitted to being a Jew, so I worried that it was a test to see if I were really a Buddhist.

"Thanks to be out of jail? Thanks to be going home?" I asked.

Tevi charming one of the police matrons while we were under house arrest in Penang Malaysia, 1997. *The Carole J. Garrison Family Archive.*

"Yes," The Chief answered. "We will go to the airport after you pray. I am waiting for the call. As soon as I receive it, this plan will be final. Go pray."

I didn't argue. Holding Tevi, I walked into the pagoda, lit incense and made three deep bows, careful not to blow on the incense—a dead giveaway that I was a fraud. Afterward, walking out of the temple, I watched The Chief's drawn face as he continued to wait for his cell phone to ring. I was barely breathing.

I saw the news on his face. Broadly smiling, The Chief signaled for us to come. Teng had gone for the car, and soon we were riding through the resort town of Penang to our small hotel to collect our luggage and leave for the airport. The world slowly returned to color and objects began to take on familiar shapes, although they were still somewhat blurred. Less than an hour later, I was purchasing our tickets to Singapore and tucking them away in the safety of my purse.

The plane wouldn't board for two more hours, and I was still officially under arrest. As my mask of strength and infallibility slipped away, The Chief looked at me as if he were seeing someone new. My eyes flickered wildly, and my face sagged with exhaustion and tension. His disappointment was obvious, but he was not unkind. Over lunch he confided that it was the young, scornful sergeant at the airport who had worked throughout my first night in custody to get us out of jail. He had also been the one to confirm that I could catch a flight to Singapore. Because he was off-duty now, I would never get to thank him.

I HAD ARRIVED IN MALAYSIA with a six-year-old orphan, ten thousand dollars in U.S. money and an unregistered hand gun. I was about to board a plane out of the country with my adopted daughter, ten thousand dollars, my life and no pistol. The Chief had taken a flyer on me, as I had on him. Our gambles had paid off.

Teng brought Tevi over from the kids' play area signaling it was time to say goodbye. Knowing that I could not hug a Muslim man, I shook his hand and then The Chief's. Then I turned and, holding Tevi close, walked through the gate. I wanted to run. No, I wanted to run and slam the airplane door tightly shut behind me. I didn't look back. I couldn't look back.♦

ROAD CLOSINGS AND U-TURNS

Preface

The moments in my life that I remember most vividly are the "aha" moments—those which stop you in your tracks, gut punch you, and force you to reconsider what you know and don't know. These moments are life's epiphanies when you become the student, rather than the teacher. ■

CHAPTER 1

The Procedure

LEERING, GHOULISH FACES SWAM in and out of my vision. "She's a druggie," I heard someone say. I felt a kick to my side.

The last thing I remembered was searching for a place to sit… I saw a phone booth but when I stumbled over, it had no seat. I leaned, breathing heavily against the booth's door frame as a thick veil of sweat soaked through my clothing. I looked desperately across the great expanse of Union Station's center hall for Frank. Finally I saw him at the ticket windows. I dropped like a stone.

I felt myself cradled in strong arms, almost tenderly and heard Frank's familiar voice shoeing people away. "You okay?"

"Do I look okay? What took you so long?"

"There was a long line for tickets to Long Island. Sorry."

He sounded sincere, protective and caring. But it wouldn't last. I did what needed to be done. The question was, would he do what he needed to get done? It still wouldn't be enough. I couldn't worry about that now. We would stay with a friend and return home to Florida in the morning.

On the train ride out to Montauk, we didn't talk much. He told me he had gone to Central Park and watched kids sailing toy boats; he didn't ask again if I was feeling okay, didn't want to know about the procedure. I stared out the train window, watching as we rolled past small dingy towns and featureless open fields; I thought about what had led up to this train ride.

My breasts had become tender and enlarged. It didn't make sense; the baby had quit nursing weeks ago. I checked my symptoms in my home first aid book. Convinced I had advanced stage breast cancer, I called my OBGYN for the first available appointment.

"You really need to get rid of that damn book," the doctor scolded. You don't have breast cancer—congratulations, you're pregnant.

Stupefied, I shook my fist at him. "I begged you to tie my tubes when the baby was born. You knew my marriage was shaky. How's another infant in the house going to help?"

"Now, now, maybe it will bring you some luck. And besides, you're young and you need your husband's permission for me to tie your tubes. He wasn't there when the baby was born."

"Fuck that! You need to fix this—now."

"I can't. Abortions aren't legal in Florida."

"They must be legal somewhere."

The doctor paused, sighed shrugging his shoulders and said, "New York City. I can put you in contact with a reputable women's clinic there. Go soon, don't wait."

Frank's body deflated when I told him about the pregnancy after dinner. He looked at me hopelessly. He didn't say it, but I knew. He was already straining at the leash with two kids and a stay at home wife. We were a burden, a responsibility he no longer wanted to bear. Another child would be another nail in his coffin.

"Mom said she would watch the girls if we went to New York together. I'll have an abortion if you promise to get a vasectomy. I'm not doing this alone."

Friggin coward, I thought. Can't ask for a divorce, can't commit to the marriage either. I should ask for a sports car or something. At this point he'd give me anything to make this go away.

Franklin went into marriage counseling, but he never had the promised vasectomy. His shrink said it would be bad for his self-image. We managed another six months of marriage until his girlfriend got pregnant.

I wish I had as vivid a memory of my daughters' birth as I do about my procedure.♦

CHAPTER 2

And the Truth Will Set You Free

THE CHINESE LIKE TO SAY THAT *bad things are the mother of good things.* At the top of the list of well-meaning platitudes provided us by the gurus and life coaches is *don't mourn the past, but embrace the future.* Appalling, I thought, when the divorce lawyer congratulated me. I was agoraphobic for months after my divorce until the director of the county's women's detention center prevailed on me to teach a weekly rug hooking class to inmates, an irony not lost on my students.

"You must show up. They will be waiting for you, and if you don't come, they'll take their frustration out on the guards and staff—it won't be pretty," she cautioned sternly when I agreed to take on the class.

Dutifully, I drove to the detention center each week. The women, mostly larcenists and prostitutes, serving misdemeanor sentences were mixed in with a few hard-core felons finishing the last months of their prison terms. We shared *my* cigarettes. I was threatened out of more than one pair of earrings and one day narrowly escaped being punctured by a metal punch hook—the inmate was having a bad day.

It was an odd cure for agoraphobia, an anxiety disorder born out of depression and fear, but once I started visiting the inmates, I began going other places as well. My life took on a new sense of purpose and possibility. In those early days, the mental image of the women locked in their cells would fill my mind. They couldn't go anywhere. My prison had been self-imposed; theirs was not. Who knew the factors that led them to their fate…what slender shred of difference and fortune separated their lives from mine. The only traveling they could do was in their imagination—my travels were only limited by my imagination. I had only lost one imagined future; there were limitless futures awaiting me.

But I'm ahead of my story. I had no inkling of where my future was heading, how those few weeks with those women would shape the rest of my life…

FRANKLIN HUGGED ME TIGHTLY, desperately, as he came through the front door, and then broke off suddenly to inspect our two-year-old daughter as if to reassure himself she was really okay.

Sitting across the dinner table, I told him it must have been an oil slick that caused the balding tires on my mother's car to plane. In that split second hanging between comprehension and disbelief, I knew I couldn't regain control of the car, but everything had felt like it was happening in stop motion—one excruciating frame after another. I was in the far left lane. Driven by an instinct, I understood that crossing the median into four lanes of oncoming traffic would mean certain death for us as well as others. Unable to draw breath, I had pulled the wheel as hard as I could, forcing the car towards the right and squeezed my eyes shut.

"The trooper said I hit a break-away post which deflected the car away from the overpass and we rolled down the embankment instead," I said with some satisfaction. The rest of dinner was uneventful and Franklin excused himself and went to our bedroom while I cleaned up and did the dishes, willing away a mental replay of events which could have cost the lives of my mother and my baby girl. Just as I was finishing the phone rang.

"Want to go to the mall for a while and forget your near death experience?" My best friend Liz asked.

"Yeah, that may be a good idea. Franklin is kind of quiet, and the baby is sleeping. I'll just ask him, but come pick me up. I should be ready in ten."

Franklin was stretched out on the bed. "Mind if I go out to the mall with Liz for an hour? I think it will help calm me down. Samantha is down for the count and should be fine."

"Sit down for a minute. I want to talk."

"Okay," I said sitting down, thinking he just wanted to offer me some comfort after my harrowing accident.

There was no preamble, no easing into his next words to me. "I want a divorce."

Just as in the midst of the accident, I was unable to draw a breath or utter a sound.

"I want a divorce. All afternoon I kept thinking about how your death would have freed me. I know it's awful, but that's what I was imagining. So, I think we should get a divorce."

If given the choice at that moment, I would have chosen death. How could I have known that moment began a chain of events that would set me free? ♦

CHAPTER 3

Neighbors

IN THE MOVIE *BELL BOOK AND CANDLE*, James Stewart is forced to drink a duck-poop green witch's brew to free himself from a love spell. He can hardly make himself bring the steaming cup to his lips.

Although the bone china cup was filled with rich, freshly brewed coffee rather than a green witch's brew, I just couldn't drink from it. A slice of oven-warmed Sarah Lee coffee cake lay uneaten on the rose-patterned china dessert dish placed before me. Sitting with me at the French provincial dining table were the newest residents of the Village of Kendale. In my role as president of its homeowners' association, I was ostensibly visiting their home to welcome them to the neighborhood—but in reality, I had been sent to check them out.

This gracious couple was not atypical of the people moving into our community. He was the new president of the recently opened South Dade Community College and, from what I could tell, she was a homemaker. What was different? They were black.

I was not happy with this assignment, scoping out new neighbors because the community was up in arms about their property values plummeting due to "integration." However, a few moments of interaction or reflection notwithstanding, I had grown up in a world of white privilege where racism was so prolific, it was in the very air we breathed. I felt queasily nauseous when trying to drink the coffee or eat the cake, not because I was ashamed but because I was afraid.

While listening to the pleasant chatter of this lovely couple, the fear evaporated. He, who held a PhD, probably had more intellectual prowess than all of my neighbors put together. She was courteous and sophisticated. They were accused of toppling home prices because of their skin color. I was a jerk.

Yes, I am Jewish, so I knew a little about discrimination, about marginalization—even back then. But I don't wear a yellow Star of David on my sleeve. No one knows I am Jewish unless I tell them my religion, announce it, and embrace it.

I sipped my coffee. I took a bite of the coffee cake, and then another. They relaxed; we smiled at each other. I welcomed them to the neighborhood. I was sincere.

At the next homeowners' association meeting, I resigned.♦

CHAPTER 4

Sex Slaves

W HAT ARE YOU STUDYING at university?" the man on the
bus asked politely from across the aisle.

He must have noticed the megaton of textbooks, bent file
folders and binders, and papers stacked helter-skelter on my lap.
I looked up from the notes I was reviewing, annoyed at being
interrupted, and gave him my best "don't bother me" look. It was
a long bus ride across town from campus to my apartment, my
kids would expect dinner and probably help with their homework, and I had to prepare for a midterm by noon the next day.
Divorced, back in school after two decades and struggling to
find my footing in a chaotic world, I was feeling overwhelmed
and pessimistic.

The man looked apologetic, and a mix of chagrin and guilt
rose hot in my cheeks. "Sorry, I don't mean to be rude. I'm
getting a doctorate in Corrections Administration." Then the
devil seized me and spat out these words into the man's kindly,

unsuspecting face: "I'm going to run an all-male, high-security prison where the men will be my sex slaves."

The signal rope was pulled, the bell sounded, the bus stopped, and the kindly man hurried off without looking back. ◆

CHAPTER 5
Busted

"DR. G, D'YA KNOW, YOU'RE RACIST." Her head tilted slightly, but she looked straight at me, didn't flinch. Her dark eyes didn't avert my return glare.

"Now why would you come back here after class and say that to me?"

"That story you told us. Don't you know what the story said to our class?"

My shoulders bounced up and down, then, feeling lopsided, I rocked on my heels. I opened and closed my mouth before asking, "The true story from my days on the Atlanta Bureau of Police; that killing, even a legitimate police killing, was a painful and chilling experience; that the officers who shot and killed a perp in the commission of a crime were not emotionally unscathed from their action; that justified shoot or not, they had to process and recover? I said it wasn't a turkey shoot, they had taken a life."

I was never happier than when I was in the classroom, University of Akron, OH, circa 1980s. *The Carole J. Garrison Family Archive.*

Carole's student, Veronica Brown (now Brown-Sims) circa 1980s University of Akron. *The Carole J. Garrison Family Archive.*

Keeping connected, Glen Stephens, Carole and Veronica Brown-Sims at a private reunion dinner, Akron Ohio, 2016. *The Carole J. Garrison Family Archive.*

"Yeah, that too. But what I, Glen—and all those white students—heard was White folks were good and cops and Black folks were robbers and crooks."

I thought hard for a moment. Yes, I had said White officers were behind the two way glass, part of the stake-out teams covering local convenient stores. Yes, I had said the Black man stood pointing a sawed-off shotgun at the cashier. Yes, I had said that the White officers' faces cracked into fine lines like a piece of broken porcelain.

Guilty as charged. My emotions toggled from anger to feeling deflated. I was incredulous that Veronica had confronted me—called me out. I was a good teacher, I cared. Block by block I built an emotional fence to protect me from her accusations.

Veronica's face softened. There was no anger in her eyes, no challenge on her lips. She looked at me expectantly and then I knew: the emotional tsunami that was swamping me was because I had let her down.

"Do you really think I'm a racist?"

"Naw, if I thought you were, I wouldn't have said anything."◆

CHAPTER 6

Realizing A Slow Death

I T WAS 1995. AKRON, OHIO'S MUSEUM OF ART was a book-
end to an aging and deteriorating downtown. But the museum
managed to thrive, bringing in both modern classical art and
more edgy contemporary political statement art. The museum
was hosting a traveling art show called "Vietnam." It comprised
mixed media from returning American vets, Vietnamese war
refugees, and Vietnamese soldiers doing art in-country during
and after the ravages of the war.

As I read about the exhibition, I could almost hear the familiar
"Wop-Wop-Wop-Wop" sound that accompanied the television
news images that bombarded my generation from the mid 1960s
into the early 1970s, as news anchors and reporters kept me
riveted to the Vietnam War. It was a pivotal time in my life
journey. It influenced critical decisions to stay in school, marry
my boyfriend so he could avoid the draft, and to have children.

By the mid-1990s, the soldiers had been forgotten, and
the memories of student protest had slipped from America's

consciousness, and I was teaching my standard Ethics in Criminal Justice course for sophomores and juniors in the Criminal Justice program at the local university. My objective was to convince my skeptical students that we are informed by at least three forms of information: sensory, cognitive, and emotional. And to really understand our position, reactions and feelings that inform our decision making—we need to tap into all three sources of reality. I decided to take the students to see the new art exhibit at the museum.

My students trooped along behind me like a group of ducklings as we headed off from campus down the broad main street several blocks to the museum. The weather was warm and sunny with a promise of an early spring. The class was ready to go, even to an art museum to see something arty about a war they didn't care about, if it meant getting out of the windowless classroom and out into the fresh air. I came up with a simple mechanism to help them distinguish between feeling or emotional reaction and cognitive processing of information. When we reached the foyer of the museum I gave each student a 3 x 5 index card and a pencil.

"Ok, you are going up to the second floor. Use the elevators inside the double doors please," I instructed.

"Hold on, there's more," I said as several boys were already rushing the big glass doors to be first in and undoubtedly with hopes of being the first out. After all, to them Vietnam was ancient history—useless and stale.

"When you finish touring the exhibit I want you to write two things," I went on, while keeping an eye out for more escape attempts. "On one side of your index card write a sentence about what you think of the exhibit—you know things like good art, not art, well crafted, I don't understand what the artist was trying to convey—that kind of stuff. On the other side, write a sentence about how the exhibit makes you feel, an emotional response, like it made me sad, or I can feel the anger in the artist's work."

Some of the students nodded, others looked at me blankly.

"Can we go now?" asked one of the boys who had tried to escape earlier. "Yes, and try not to be rowdy—indoor voices and all that good stuff, right?" I said as they began to disappear through the glass doors and into the opening elevator.

I stood by the front door 35 or 40 minutes later to collect the cards as each student left to return to campus. They came in small groups: some thanked me, others just tossed me the card, and a few made comments about the exhibit. Sarah was almost the last to leave. She handed me the card but hardly met my gaze.

"You okay?" I asked, not really very concerned, and taking her index card and putting it somewhere in the stack. "Yeah," she replied noncommittally. "Here's the assignment. Thanks for bringing us here. I don't think I would have come otherwise."

After she left I stayed back—they didn't need me to chaperone their way back to campus—and began thumbing through the cards.

"Wow, good stuff." "I liked the caskets in the mirror case, it was cool." "I didn't understand what a lot of it meant. I don't know much about that war."

Then I picked up Sarah's card. One side was blank. I turned it over and read, "Now I know why my dad committed suicide."

In that moment, the years and the generational divide evaporated. Momentarily stunned by what I had read, I finally ran after her, hoping I could catch her before she was gone. I found Sarah, about three blocks from the museum. She was walking alone, slow enough that catching up to her was not difficult.

"Sarah," I caught her by the arm and she turned to face me. "I read your feeling comment. Do you want to talk about it?" I asked, trying to cajole her but not force it. We lost over 58,000 American lives to the Vietnam War, and 100,000 or more to suicide — and most of those occurred after the men came home.

"It's okay," she said looking up the street and not directly at me. "I don't remember much about my dad. I was little when he came home from the war. My mom told me he became totally troubled, took drugs, and drank a lot. I think he was suffering from the war, but my mom couldn't stand it and divorced him. After my mom took me and left, he committed suicide."

Then turning and looking directly at me she said, "But, Doctor G, I thought it was my mom's fault my dad killed himself. I always hated him for making her unhappy, and her for leaving him. But now I think I understand. It was the war that killed him—it just killed him slower."

I hadn't paid much attention to Sarah before that day at the museum. Now, I will never forget her.♦

CHAPTER 7

The Bonus

W E HAVE ENOUGH LAWYERS in the family...and besides, you don't like to read."

My brother Nat, a law professor at Emory, had advised me to get a PhD instead of a law degree. I took his sage advice, left the police department, got my doctorate, taught criminal justice and, for a time, served as the director of a women's studies program. His wife Libby, who got no such advice, went to law school, clerked for the Ninth Circuit Court of Appeals and became a corporate attorney for Coca-Cola.

One December morning during my stint in women's studies, the office phone rang. My sister-in-law Libby's voice sounded frustrated and indignant. "Carole, I need your advice. I don't think that Coke plans to give me a Christmas bonus equivalent to my male colleagues."

"No ultimatums," I advised "If you threaten to quit and the corporate bosses don't give you an equal bonus, you had better be sure you really want to quit. If you don't make good on your threat, they would own you."

"I'll think about it," she said. The phone clicked off and I resumed my work.

The holidays came and went. A news article in early January on gender pay inequality reminded me of our conversation. Libby hadn't called, so I called her.

"How did the bonus thing go?" I asked.

"No problem. There was parity. It's all good. I took your advice."

"Just out of curiosity, what was your bonus, if you don't mind telling me?" Libby's reply made me gasp.

"Thanks. Can I speak to my brother for a minute?"

Nat came to the phone. "Hi, sis. What's up?"

"Remind me, brother dear, never again to take your advice."

Libby's bonus was more than my annual salary.♦

Weaving Women's Colors

THE INTRICATELY BEADED AND EMBROIDERED Palestinian nomad's dress laid heavily on my shoulders and was even a greater burden emotionally. I was surprised by its weight upon my body and my spirit. I choose to wear it to open the June 1990, National Women's Studies Conference: Weaving Women's Colors on the campus of the University of Akron. My goal was to use the symbolism of the dress worn by women, many of whom were sworn enemies of Israel and Jews, as a statement of solidarity with women around the globe.

I was finishing my introductory remarks to the welcoming ceremonies, relieved and quite proud of myself in my Palestinian nomad dress, when a small group of women approached the podium. One woman stepped up onto the stage, grabbing the microphone and attempting to wrest it from me.

My back stiffened, my face tightened till it was taut and hard. I tightened my grip on the microphone and pulled back. My impulse was to turn off the mike—to fight back harder, but I didn't. Instead, I looked into her angry face, her brown skin shiny with perspiration, and I stopped struggling. I handed her the microphone and she and her colleagues took the stage, challenging the white, mostly middle-class academics who ran the NWSA.

"The national leadership perpetuates the same administration and system of oppression that you are supposedly trying to eliminate. You care more about day care, scholarship and salaries than ending sexism and by extension, racism." Her voice, loud, clear and passionate, rang out across the stunned audience.

The conference split along lines of class, race and sexuality.

Ultimately, the caucuses representing poor and working-class women, lesbian women and women of color, along with Women Studies staff, left the conference early.

.

There is no real tribe that includes all women simply because they are women. ♦

A Seat At the Table

I SUFFERED FROM A PARTICULARLY NASTY combination of impulsivity, which was followed by acute feelings of recrimination and guilt — all settling down to simmering anger. If I were to hazard a guess, I would say that this affliction was the result of arrested development caused by my inability to let go of the hurt and anger from an experience with childhood sexual abuse, the premature death of my father, and failed relationships.

I was raised in the perpetual American summertime of the 1950s, in a population hiding from both the traumatic past of WWII and searching for ways to cope with the social unrest and technological changes that were coming with the Vietnam War. Like many who grew up in that era, I was restless for change but still tethered to conventionality by self-doubt.

It didn't help that I was Jewish. My insecurity was rooted in more than just having a Jewish mother; there was an unspoken consciousness among Jews of being "other," of being at risk. I experienced marginalization as a child in public school, tasked to do the Christmas and Easter bulletin boards — decorations which never reflected any other celebrations of the seasons.

The American public schools were ruthless socialization apparatuses, ethnic cleansing machines all supported by the mythology of the public good. I embraced cultural assimilation and got on with my life, confusing loss of identity with secular humanism. I became a holiday Jew. But I was to be painfully reminded of what it meant to be born a Jew as an adult.

Diversity and Education — that was the name of California's teachers' association conference. "Dr. Garrison, Women's Studies, University of Akron, "We would like you to facilitate a group of Jewish teachers," the invitation said. Why me? I wondered aloud. A call from a former colleague answered the why. She was the organizer, and I was her pick. I thought her choice was my only credential other than a long lineage of Jewish grandmothers extending back generations.

California was warm and sunny, the conference room large and tense. The topic had become increasingly personal, and even before the teachers, all of whom were women, were divided up by their self-identified ethnicity for the break-out sessions, many had already shifted tables and chairs, re-grouping themselves with others who had chosen the same classification. All but the Jewish teachers. When I called them for the break-out session, they came from multiple groups seated in the room. A reminder of the ability, the desire to pass.

The tension from the big room rolled in with them into the small conference room. Fifteen women sat mute around the shiny cherry table, each looking furtively from one to another.

"Um, hi. I'm Carole Garrison, your facilitator. Uh, you don't know me, I'm from Ohio, but I assume you know each other."

"California is a big state." Came the reply tainted in sarcasm and rebellion.

Fuck, I thought. "Let's start by going 'round the table and introducing ourselves. I'll start. I'm Carole Gozansky Garrison."

The room felt warmer.

"Can we now, maybe, each share a story about ourselves?" I started with my Christmas bulletin board story. The others jumped in, eagerly sharing similar stories—all but one woman who stayed silent. I looked directly at her, challenging, her encouraging her if possible, to share a story.

"I am the daughter of Holocaust survivors. We don't talk about such things. We don't publicize our heritage. We don't trust God to protect us, even here."

The chill that swept through the room was not one of rebellion, but one of grief, a shared recognition deep in our collective consciousness that whether we were American-born or the children of labor camp survivors, we had an intense fear of confronting our Christian peers about the lack of inclusiveness in American schools.

The group came up with a few suggestions based on past experiences to make schools more inclusive: use seasonal titles like winter and spring for holiday breaks rather than Christmas and Easter; include more diversity in holiday program recognizing the many traditions outside Christianity; include secularism and atheism in curriculum about belief systems; make Jewish holidays part of the main menu, not just one of many desserts.

"Okay, good suggestions, nothing too radical but straight forward and easy to implement. Who wants to present them?"

Nothing, a cold silence fell around the table until one woman spoke up. "You do it. You're going back to Ohio—you've got nothing to fear."

Not my job. I sat silent. How much was my honorarium for this gig? Not enough.

"We can't do it…we won't do it."

I had felt the same connection, the same fear, and dread that had run like an electric circuit through the group earlier. The room pulsed with collective palpable fear. Reluctantly I said "Okay."

We returned to join the larger group in the main hall. This time the fifteen women sat together at two adjoining tables. All fifteen pair of eyes were on me when I took the podium to report the break-out group's ideas. I started.

I barely noticed the first of the women leave her seat to walk over and stand next to me. Then it was two. The daughter of survivors came next. By the time I began suggestion three, all fifteen women stood on either side of the podium.

For centuries the marginalized, the weak have accommodated those in power for the sake of peace — not out of the goodness of their hearts or because it was the right thing to do. But the time comes to make their experiences and preferences known, to take their seat at the table. That moment had come for those women.♦

CHAPTER 10

The Last to Know

IT WAS AROUND 7:30 P.M. when I got home. Dusk was falling and the house was dark. I had expected Mike, my partner for the past decade, to be home, but there was no sign of his presence, no green twenty-year-old Mustang in the carport.

The red light on the answering machine pulsed urgently in the dark, beckoning me to attend to it immediately. I switched on the hall light, dropped my keys into the small glass lotus-shaped bowl on the antique cherry end table and punched the play button.

A loud beep preceded a perky female voice. "Dr. Lee, Mike, it's Tasha from the realty office. The one-bedroom apartment that you inquired about is now available for immediate occupancy. Just stop by the rental office, drop off your deposit and pick up the keys. I know you'll love it."

"Life can change in the blink of an eye." Or, in this case the blink of a light.◆

Synchronicity

LIVES CAN BE SUMMED UP AS the result of choices we make or as a series of events that seem less about choice and more about happenings—random, unlooked for, unplanned. I imagine that many people would call what happened to me within a four-year period an example of God's plan. Carl Jung would have called it synchronicity: events are "meaningful coincidences" if they occur with no causal relationship yet seem to be meaningfully related. I call it my very lucky life.

> *1988:* In a surprise and unorthodox move by its organizing committee, I was appointed founding director of the Women's Studies program at the University of Akron. As this was not my academic discipline, I continued to teach Criminal Justice courses as well as develop the new program—creating an unexpected synergy among my feminist activism, my research on women in policing and my applied ethics classes within the Criminal Justice curriculum.

1989: Not since riding the "scream machine" at Six Flags had I been as terrified as I felt taking my Criminal Justice students to rappel off the rooftop of the University of Akron's four-story faculty parking deck. To the great delight of the ROTC's commanding officer on campus, I went first. I hate rappelling; I am phobic about edges, heights and roller coasters. So were most of the wanna-be cops. That was the point—finding the will to overcome fear.

1990: Nominated as a Distinguished Educator by the same commanding officer, I was invited to the ROTC's summer camp at Fort Knox, Kentucky. Challenged to join a visiting U.S. Army general in a rappelling exercise with the cadets, I fumbled my way through yet another terrifying afternoon, bouncing rather than leaping down the side of a tall tower. That evening I sat with the general for dinner. Over an otherwise pleasant meal, he critiqued my attempt to rappel and assured me that I had the worse form he had ever observed.

1990: Several months later, to my astonishment, I received a phone call from the Pentagon. I had been appointed to a three-year term on the Defense Advisory Committee on Women in the Services, known as DACOWITS, by Secretary of Defense Dick Cheney. Only later did I learn that my appointment was based upon the recommendation of the Army general who had recently critiqued my rappelling form at Fort Knox. One of only five non-political appointees, I was the Army's pick.

To some extent, this little series of events has influenced the rest of my life, as well as much of what is written in this memoir.♦

DACOWITS and Regrets

HELLO, DR. GARRISON. This is the Pentagon calling from Secretary Cheney's office."

"Whatever joke you're playing, it's not funny," I replied. I put the receiver back in its cradle, shaking my head. The phone rang again.

"Dr. Garrison, please don't hang up. You have been nominated by the Secretary of Defense to serve on the DACOWITS."

"Excuse me, the what?"

"The - Defense - Advisory - Committee - on - Women - in - the - Services." The man spoke each word slowly and deliberately.

He sounded serious and legitimate, but why would Dick Cheney, a man I had little affection for, pick me for anything? Had I not joined a protest march only a few weeks ago, holding up a sign saying, "Let the Pentagon have a bake sale, while Congress funds the Department of Education."

Announcement for a talk on the challenges of returning active service military women and PTSD at West Virginia State College, spring 2013. *The Carole J. Garrison Family Archive.*

DACOWITS Executive Board, U.S. Department of Defense, 1993. *The Carole J. Garrison Family Archive.*

WHILE SERVING ON THE DACOWITS in the very early 1990s, I was beguiled by women pilots who returned from Desert Storm with tales of flying in combat; I was thrilled to fly over the Grand Canyon in an airborne tanker with an all-female crew to refuel a jet fighter piloted by women. The women wanted the same perks of their service as the men received, but policymakers like Dick Cheney and Colin Powell weren't interested in sharing them. I became emotionally hooked into their cause following a visit to Paris Island, where I witnessed the training of female Marines.

"General, why don't the women throw loaded grenades during training?" I asked the middle-aged male Marine sitting across from me.

"To reduce the likelihood of their blowing anyone up if they don't throw far enough," he replied with perfect candor.

I flashed back to my days in the police academy. The few women in my class sat around watching the men spar and fight as they practiced boxing and unarmed physical defensive tactics. We weren't allowed to participate in either. "Might get hurt, might kick some guy in the groin," the training lieutenant explained. The lesson was clear. We couldn't defend ourselves. We were unqualified. The male Marines were teaching their female counterparts the same lesson by permitting them to throw only dud grenades—you can't do it.

The general and I debated the issue until, finally, his composure in doubt and his cheeks reddening, he leaned over the table till his face was only a foot away from mine. "Why do you hate women so much that you would send them into harm's way?"

"Why do you hate men so much that you would make them carry this burden alone?"

I HELPED TO DRAFT THE REPEAL of the Women in Combat exclusionary rule. Congress passed a partial repeal based on the proposed legislation submitted by DACOWITS. Rather than taking pride in our legislative success on behalf of the servicewomen who were already serving in the theater of war without acknowledgment for their combat roles, an inner turmoil erupted. A debate raged inside my head.

Women should do whatever they want and are capable of doing.

What about the women who joined the military, never expecting to be drafted into combat and not wanting to be fighters?

This repeal will help to compensate the courageous women who serve in combat but are denied the credit and rewards associated with their valor.

Why am I supporting the war machine?

Patriarchy and male privilege were sustained and empowered by a "warrior class mentality" that women were excluded from joining.

Why am I encouraging women to join an inhumane, antiquated methodology for solving the world's problems?

Why not fight for women to be equally valued for their contributions, from raising babies to keeping the economy and society on an even keel, rather than support the notion that warriors perform the most valued role in society?

ON JANUARY 23, 2013, then-Secretary of Defense Leon Panetta rescinded the final ban on women serving in ground combat units and set forth a plan to implement this policy change, so my terrible conundrum effectively became a moot point. Nevertheless, I have fretted about my participation in this repeal ever since.

With fewer options to effect change, all I can do now is use whatever forums are available to champion understanding and support for our returning veterans, female and male, who come home debilitated by post-traumatic stress—from whatever trauma they endured.♦

CHAPTER 13
The Kindness of Strangers

SOME YEARS AGO, 1979 to be exact, I lived in a small predominantly white upper middle-class New Jersey community bordering the then prestigious Bell Laboratories, New Providence. I taught public administration and criminal justice at Kean College. My teenage daughter, Debra, was attending boarding school in Vermont, and coming home by train for the Thanksgiving holiday, and I was picking her up at the station in downtown Newark, New Jersey. With my nine-year-old daughter, Samantha, securely fastened to my hand, we climbed the stairs to the platform to await the train. Newark at the time was a city with a reputation for crime and violence, and I felt uncomfortable, if not afraid, among the throngs of train station denizens and the large number of African Americans departing and arriving. I clutched my daughter tightly and waited as the train pulled into the station.

Debra arrived dragging what looked like a dozen large duffel bags. I could only imagine she brought home everyone's laundry or every item she owned for the weekend. I couldn't imagine how I was going to get off the platform and downstairs to a trolley while securing my nine-year-old, my purse, my teenager and her mountain of duffel bags.

Just then a large, neatly dressed, African American man came over and asked if I needed help. Holding my hand up as if to stop him, I said, "No thanks, we can manage." I pulled both my daughters and my purse closer to me. But as I looked around it was obvious that I couldn't manage, and I turned back to the man and said, "Please, yes, I do need some help." Wordlessly, he proceeded to sweep up Samantha, most of the duffel bags and headed down the stairs—Debra and I closely on his heels, dragging the rest of her belongings.

As we came down the stairs, a woman and three children were looking up smiling and waving in our direction. The man helping me was grinning back, unable to wave given all he was carrying. Our small band of informal porters reached the trolleys at the bottom of the stairs. He quickly unloaded his bundles and Samantha only to be crushed by his own family as they rushed to greet him. I called to him before he got away, "I don't know how to thank you."

He turned momentarily from his reunion and said "Don't thank me, just pass it on."

Shame and guilt mingled together in a stew of remorse. This wasn't the first time I felt fear among people of color—made wrong assumptions, and it wasn't the first time I was found lacking.

What really angered me was how hard it was to learn the lesson—goodness wasn't the province of white people.♦

The Waiting Room

I BARELY NOTICED THE OTHER WOMEN sitting in chairs alongside each wall of the reception area. I hated this exam. I was anxious on the drive to my appointment, daunted by the parking garage at the clinic, and nervous while doing the paperwork and waiting for my name to be called. The staff and nurses were all perky and the reception area was pleasant, with cheerful wallpaper and sugary artwork—but the little side tables held stacks of pamphlets on breast cancer, its causes and treatments. None of which made me happier to be there.

The sound of my name, like a bellowing gong, brought me out of my fretful stupor and into a state of wakefulness. How many times had I done this? Two dozen? Maybe more. And yet I quailed at the mere idea of walking back to the examination area.

I glanced over at the women sitting in the interior room—not looking at faces, but rather for an empty seat. Taking one, I sat in silence and waited. The magazines were *Southern Living, Women's Day* and *Health and Fitness.* No racy tabloids like at the beauty salon. I pretended to flip through some recipes. Gong! My name rang out again. No one looked up as I entered through the door marked "Examination Rooms."

The smiling nurse showed me to a small changing closet where I robotically undressed, rubbed my underarms with a wipe, took off my jewelry and dropped it into my purse. Gathering up my clothes, I pushed them into a cubby and followed the nurse—her smile still pasted on her face—to the next room in the process. The technician apologized for cold hands, and we completed the usual routine.

"Please get dressed and have a seat outside," she said. "The nurse will let you know when the radiologist gives us the all clear. Just a few more minutes, dear."

I had always understood Einstein's theory of relativity metaphorically. For example, time flies by when you're busy, as it does when you're late for a flight or an important meeting. At the gym, on the other hand, time creeps along as if the hands of the clock were weighted down with the menacing barbells being lifted by the grunting, tattooed musclemen. And time also crawls on a Sunday afternoon when you have nothing to do, or while you're waiting for the dinner guests to arrive long after everything has finished cooking. But never does time go more slowly than when you're waiting for a nurse to give you thumbs up from a radiologist.

"Ms. Johnson, you can get dressed now," the nurse called from a crack in the door. A lady sighed loudly, color flushing into her gray cheeks. She got up and moved, almost at a run, toward the dressing room—not waiting around for another announcement from the nurse, saying she had mistakenly told the lady she could dress.

Chill bumps appeared on my arms, although the room was stuffy. I stared at my watch again, but only three minutes had passed since the last time I'd checked it. I bit my cuticle, watching the expanding red blossom as my nail bled. Eventually I began to observe the other women with me in the room—each one deep in her own thoughts, face blank, hands folded in her lap or across her chest—as if protecting her breasts from any bad news. White faces grayed, and brown faces turned dusky and pale when someone was summoned back to the examining rooms. I continued to sit and wait as time dawdled onward.

"Ms. Garrison?" A blank expression replaced the nurse's fixed smile. "Carole? Please come back with me. The radiologist wants just one more look."

Time did not move again for a very long while—three more months until I got a thumbs-up.♦

LESSONS FROM ROADS LESS TRAVELED

Preface

Luck and a severe case of directional dyslexia have combined to make most of my days an adventure. When I was a school girl, getting off a bus on the wrong corner would send me walking unfamiliar streets to Chicago's Union Station rather than to the Art Institute for Saturday classes. I might have been late for my art lesson, but I almost always discovered a new deli or some interesting characters as I sought help to get myself pointed in the right direction. I am most happy when I am wandering around, usually lost, in some foreign country where my travels reveal secrets not only about new and interesting places and people, but the ones that lead to new discoveries about myself. ∎

CHAPTER 1

Traveling Alone, Lonely Traveling

I ARRIVED IN SAIGON (Ho Chi Minh City) with few compli-
cations other than an extra hour at the Cambodian border
because some lump head on the bus didn't have his visa with
him. Cambodia's border guards spent their days lazing in
cement huts, about one hundred yards from three brand-new
enormous casinos, or trying to exploit unaware travelers who
got caught in the web of official and unofficial customs regula-
tions—anything that would net them an extra twenty dollars
from the vulnerable.

Straddling the border on the other side was Vietnam, which
had a proper customs building with a modern luggage-scanning
machine. After passing through that checkpoint, you knew you
were in another country—one with good roads, factories, and
electricity lines. Of course, seeing the huge spires of Catholic
churches in every hamlet took some getting used to after Cambodia, where the only steeples rising loftily into the firmament
were atop Buddhist temples.

The thrill of adventure, of being on my own in Vietnam for two weeks, was at once both exhilarating and terrifying—exactly what I wanted. The Mekong Express bus finally pulled into Phạm Ngũ Lão Street.

No driver stood waiting at the Saigon bus terminal with my name reassuringly printed in large, easy-to-read letters on a card. Luckily I noticed a travel bureau across the street, where an employee graciously called Trong, the name on business card I had tucked away with my passport. He arrived within minutes, driving a sleek white Mercedes sedan. Unfortunately my driver spoke negligible English, so I couldn't request a pit stop or dinner, and we drove directly out of town towards the mountains shimmering green and purple on the horizon. Rather than attempt to inquire where I wanted to go, Mr. Trong had made a unilateral decision to go up into the mountains then and there. Locating a road sign we had passed on a torn and folded map I found in the glove compartment, I saw that we were headed to Dalat, in the southern part of the Central Highlands region.

At nightfall, the well-kept two-lane highway became narrow and treacherous. Trong avoided the ghost-like figures walking along the road in the darkening shadows of dusk as well as the oncoming, lumbering Russian trucks and the zigzagging, speeding motor scooters.

By eight o'clock I was in the heart-thumping, noisy mountain resort town of Dalat in full chaotic swing. Tired and hungry, I got a room and a bowl of *pho* for the grand sum of twelve dollars. My earplugs, along with Boise earphones and a meditation CD, made it possible to sleep through the din.

At 5:30 a.m. when I got up, it was early enough to see cleaners on the street sweeping up from the night before and sellers returning to their shops to open for business and remake the whole mess over again. I explored the few places along Dalat's street scene that were open and tried a cup of Vietnamese

Carole in front of the bus from Phnom Penh (Cambodia) to Ho Chi Minh City (2005). *The Carole J. Garrison Family Archive.*

Carole in posing for a snap shot in Dalat, Vietnam (2005). I probably should have chosen a different T-shirt to wear, but by then no one cared. The U.S. and Vietnam, once horrific enemies, were now trading buddies and friends. *The Carole J. Garrison Family Archive.*

coffee. No wonder they only drank it in the morning. It was lethal—damn French influence.

Using hand signs and showing him Nha Trang on the map, I eventually got Trong to understand that I wanted to leave Dalat. We were heading east in the direction of the Vietnamese coast when the Ethnic Minorities Museum caught my attention. With more hand signals, in addition to demands to "stop," I convinced Trong to turn around and take me to the museum. This was why I traveled alone—my schedule, my adventure.

The museum, housed in a huge mansion in the style of the French colonial period, was a mix of ethnic handicrafts, artifacts, and graphic photos of French exploitation of the ethnic tribes from that era. But at the top of the stairs, in the attic, were memorabilia from the Vietnam War.

Hanging on a wall under a sharply sloped eave was a startling black and white photo of an American soldier holding up his trophy—half of a Vietnamese man. The other, bottom half of him was still lying on the ground where he had been cut in two by a machine gun. Standing alone and staring at the photo in a stew of revulsion mixed with guilt, I tugged angrily at my T-shirt, emblazoned with a U.S. flag. I wanted someone to bear witness to that horror. I craved someone to hear my anguish, to share the moment with me, and to relieve me of the need to process the experience on my own.

This is why you shouldn't always travel alone; sometimes, sharing is required.♦

CHAPTER 2

She Must Be Crazy

THE DRIVER I HIRED to take me from Ho Chi Minh City up the Vietnam coast to Hu-Long Bay had let me know from the start that he was a driver, not a tour guide. That meant that, despite not liking packaged group tours in general, I had to make some exceptions to make the most of my ten-day journey.

When the Huế car-and-boat tour van left me off at my hotel, my hair was a wreck; wind and rain had done their worst grounding our pontoon dragon boat, forced off the Perfume River by a sudden, ferocious storm. A relative of the hotel's owner gave me a motor scooter ride to a local beauty shop to get my hair washed. He promised to tell my driver, Mr. Trong, where I was and send him to fetch me in an hour.

In Thailand, you get a neck massage; in Cambodia, a good head scrub; in Vietnam, you get both plus a fifteen-minute full facial. I leaned back, closed my eyes, and enjoyed the pampering—that is, until one of the girls trimmed off all of my fingernails. To this day I haven't a clue if I paid for the clipping, but I had clean hair and no fingernails, all at a cost of only seven U.S. dollars.

Trong had waited patiently for me to begin our pre-arranged excursion to Hue's petit version of Beijing's Forbidden City. When I asked him why the girl had cut off my fingernails, he replied, "Don't know," while shrugging his shoulders and putting the key in the ignition.

We drove in to the old city and stopped at a large plaza, which fronted the entrance to the Citadel and the Imperial Forbidden City. After Trong dropped me off there and went off on his own, I happily wandered through the few buildings and rooms that still remained of the palace. Structurally, the Purple Palace appeared to be a miniature of Beijing's, but there were no crowds to impede my leisurely appreciation of what was uniquely different. Although there's almost nothing left of its former opulence, and most of the pillars, carvings and walls have suffered from centuries of termite and storm damage—as well as the more disturbing destruction from American bombardment during the Vietnam War—I was still reluctant to leave at closing time.

As it was too early for dinner and two hours until Trong's scheduled return at 8:00 p.m., I took a horse-drawn rickshaw ride inside the old city that brought me back to the large plaza in front of the Citadel. Kite vendors hawked their goods, people did their tai chi exercises, and ice cream carts were parked every twenty feet or so. I bought an ice cream bar and a kite to take home as a gift, then sat down to wait for my ride.

After following me around, the thin, elderly man who had driven my rickshaw continued to pester me. Apparently he thought, or hoped, that I would eventually need him to return me to my hotel because he just couldn't grasp the fact that I was waiting for a hired car and driver.

I ignored him as a couple pushed their little girl over to talk to me. She was a small sixth grader, a shy and soft spoken only child. Her father worked in a shoe factory, and her mom stayed at home. I smiled, she smiled, and soon we managed to get a conversation going in English, which shortly turned to traveling to the moon.

When the clock tower at the end of the plaza showed only fifteen more minutes until my announced departure time, I was surrounded by a little circle of new friends who worried that I wouldn't be picked up—the little girl and her family, the rickshaw driver, a tourist photographer, and assorted others. Thinking I was confused, maybe crazy, none of them would leave me. After all, what woman travels alone, and who travels in a private car?

Of course, the old rickshaw driver was still hoping for a late evening fare although, at one point, he had offered to drive me for free at the urging of the others. But at eight o'clock on the dot, a shiny white sedan—not a taxi or a hotel van—pulled up. On impulse, I gave the kite to the little girl and shook hands with everyone, bidding farewell to about a dozen people who looked both awestruck and relieved.

The irony was not lost on me, an American visiting the half-destroyed Forbidden City in Huế thirty years after the end of the Vietnam War, that I would be afforded not just courtesy but also true concern for my well-being…and perhaps from their point of view, my sanity.♦

CHAPTER 3

An Unfinished Rivalry

I RAN MY FINGER ALONG the etched name of the last American casualties of the war engraved on the massive black granite blocks stretching for yards in both directions. "They died in Cambodia," the monument's guide said.

I came of age during the anti-war protests of the 1970s. I had a passionate dislike for Richard Nixon and his Cambodia bombing policy, breakfast-lunch-dinner, not knowing at the time the Cambodian king's complicity in Nixon's decision to carry out the B-52 raids over Cambodia's border with Vietnam. While working in SE Asia, I even went to Saigon, visited the Củ Chi tunnels where the U.S. Air Force sprayed tons of agent orange and Khmer Rouge guerillas viciously tortured U.S. ground troops, grieved for both sides in their war of mutual destruction.

As an American expat living in Cambodia in the mid-1990s, I had occasionally been brought a shoe box of remains from a local, claiming it contained the remains of a U.S. soldier MIA. "You give me dolla? I give you box." I would take the box, pay

Mr. Trong, Carole's Vietnamese driver, 2005. *The Carole J. Garrison Family Archive.*

a few U.S. dollars and carry it over to the MIA unit at the U.S. embassy for verification. If it was a confirmed MIA, I would join the formal ceremony at the Phnom Penh airport as embassy and military officials loaded the box onto a military transport back to Andrews Airforce base for final processing and burial.

IN 2005 I RETURNED TO VIETNAM, rented a car and driver, and traveled from Saigon up the coast to Halong Bay in the far north-east of the country. It was the thirtieth anniversary of the end of the war. The last leg of my journey to Vietnam was coming to an end as we drove south back to Saigon from Halong Bay in the far northeast of the country. Trong, my Vietnamese driver, stopped so I could climb up the not quite finished North Vietnam war memorial at the DMZ — the 17th parallel, north latitude. A warm breeze kissed my face where I stood eighteen stories high on a balcony of the gently swaying pagoda. The breeze was a welcome relief to the sun, which blazed overhead with only a hint of vapor-thin clouds scurrying across an intense blue sky.

I peered down on the peaceful countryside along the Beh Hai River — on the rice paddies, farmers and water buffalo. But I couldn't hear the gurgle of the river or the lowing of the buffalo. The scene was silent, and unmoving, like a postcard. The sounds of war were blanketed by time, but the sounds of life had been silenced as well.

Then, down a side road off to the left, I saw two young women riding bicycles, dressed in traditional Vietnamese *áo dài,* their long, black silky hair streaming behind them from under conical straw hats called *nón lá.* Each girl steered with one hand while clasping the other's hand with her free one. They could have been riding out of a travel video made in the 1950s, or even the 1940s.

In a different direction stood the not quite finished South Vietnam war memorial. According to the story, I had heard, every time one side declared its structure complete, the other side would add another floor.

As I looked across at the memorial, the tears started slowly. I knew the statistics. The total number of American casualties, not including the fourteen hundred still counted as MIA, was 211,454. The grand total of deaths attributed to the war in Vietnam, Cambodia and Lao was approximately 1,450,000 people.

Trong had waited for me in the car. "A lot of my friends and family died here," I said, my eyes stinging and still wet. He looked at me without changing expressions, his face blank. He repeated my words, "A lot of my friends and family died here."♦

CHAPTER 4

The Silent Scream

T HE TWO YOUNG WOMEN who met me at the Calcutta airport were the daughters of a former Indian maharaja. "Here,"
one of them said, thrusting a bag of toilet paper at me. "You'll
probably want this."

On a trip to Asia with my mom, I had left her in New Delhi
while I went to visit the sister of one of my international graduate
students back in Ohio. Although I had been introduced to Asian-
style squat toilets in South Korea and China, I wasn't prepared
for receiving a grocery bag full of toilet paper upon my arrival.

I looked at my reception committee with some surprise, but
their haughty bearing suggested that I accept their "gift" without
comment. The maharaja's daughters explained, in perfect British
English, that they had volunteered to meet me and take me to the
home of my student's sister, who was still at her law office. Load-
ing me into a yellow cab that looked like it was manufactured in
the 1960s (but was actually new in the 1980s), we lurched into

the crowded, chaotic traffic; black diesel belched from ornately decorated trucks and little motorcycle pulled tuk-tuks.

On the way, they asked what I wanted to see in Calcutta. "I'd like to see a temple to the goddess Kali," I answered. I hadn't given sightseeing much thought, but I knew about Kali, the Hindu goddess of Shakti—feminine energy, creativity and fertility—so she was the first thing that popped into my head. Besides, the black, multi-armed warrior was a fearsome creature, and I was a women's studies professor who had once been a cop. A temple in her honor seemed to be the perfect place to visit.

"Okay, we will come with our mother in the morning to take you to visit Kalighat Temple. By the way, you shouldn't wear blue sapphires, neelam, because they are under the influence of the deity Shani and they can affect your life—they are bad luck," the older sister said without taking a noticeable breath. I looked down at the birthday present I was wearing, a sapphire solitaire ring, and wondered how I had gotten stuck with these young women.

IN THE MORNING, AS PROMISED, the sisters and their mother—a genteel dark-haired woman about my age, wearing many diamonds but no sapphires—picked me up in a chauffeur-driven large black sedan. While they retained some of the trappings of their family's former wealth and status, the rest of their possessions were, for the most part, shabby chic. Unlike the yellow cab, for example, their car was actually a remnant from the sixties.

As we pulled into the parking lot adjacent to the Kalighat Temple, I could see matted-haired Hindu ascetics with painted faces and bodies sleeping against ancient walls or crouching by small smoked pots of peanuts, scattering stray dogs away. I knew they were supposed to be spiritual, but I found them terrifying—especially the one who shook his fist and yelled at me for taking his photo. My three guides seemed unconcerned and pressed through the throngs of people to the main platform, which was raised to a height of about four feet.

The dais was just as packed as the parking lot, so I could not see the shrine of Kali. Even standing on my tiptoes as close as possible to the edge, I could only glimpse the gold tip of her headdress. Fine, I thought; she wasn't my goddess. I didn't like the crowds, and the small children who were grabbing at me, touching me, and begging for rupees were beginning to make me as anxious as someone who saw a problem but felt totally helpless to solve it. I was done. I had come, had not seen, and was ready to leave.

Just then strong hands grabbed mine and lifted me onto the platform. I watched in horror as worshipers in front of me were pushed aside or shoved off the platform to make an open pathway to the fearsome image of Kali. My screams died unheard, stuck in my throat as I saw my pseudo-tour guides smile in pleasure at the sight of their mother handing rupees over to the temple priest in exchange for clearing the way for me.

Like your reaction when waking to your cat as it proudly lays the gift of a still-warm mouse or shrew on your pillow, you turn away, aghast at the sight. But what can you do? There I was, a visitor—worse, a guest who claimed to want, above all else, to see Kali—so I had no choice. Unwilling to behave like an ungrateful guest or an ugly American, I swallowed my bile, walked up to the shrine, viewed Kali's necklace of skulls, and silently wished that she would not think I had a self-centered view of the world (as I was fairly certain my hosts did).

Kali is also the goddess of death, but she brings death to the over-blown ego, not to the body.♦

CHAPTER 5

An Intervention

THE COUNTER-CULTURE IS ALIVE and well in Laos. Most T-shirts for sale along the river sport images of Jamaican Bob Marley, Cuba's Che and Vietnam's Uncle Ho or ganja. You can buy Cuban cigars and see lots of older Anglo men with young and younger Lao girls in tow.

I see a skinny old coot on a bike, dressed in baggy khaki shorts and a dirty T-shirt, his eyes are red-rimmed and glassy, and his weathered face is covered with a grayish blond stubble. He's circling a young woman walking hand in hand with a small girl. While he's moving in closer, he signals the universal hand gesture for "do you want to fuck?" The woman is dressed in a traditional sarong and modest blouse, not the seductive skinny jeans and halters preferred by women who plied their trade along Vientiane's beaches. She looks flustered, and he unwilling to halt the pursuit—and there's the kid. Walking up I take the little girl's hand and put my arm around the young woman. "Walk with me," I say, but she doesn't answer. She speaks no

English—no language is necessary. The old bastard rides off a little way beyond a stand of trees, waits, mutters and watches. I continue walking with them toward the busy avenue that borders the park.

Once we're certain that he isn't following us, we part with only a nod of the young woman's head. I watch her and the girl cross the street and head away from the river park. I have a flash of penis envy. A man would have hauled off and knocked the bastard on his scrawny old carcass—and wouldn't that feel good.♦

CHAPTER 6
The Hajj

I AM AN INFIDEL...I'm Jewish...I'm an American, and I'm a woman. Any one or all of these factors put me at risk when I visited Iran in the summer of 2004. To my Iranian friend's more religious relatives, I was an unwelcome guest.

My exclusion, however, was minimal, because most of the family embraced me warmly; and I assumed certain behaviors, which allowed me to fit into the wider community. For example, I rarely wore a hijab, head-scarf, in the house, but dutifully put one on to go outside or to any public place. I left it on when relatives came who wore their head coverings while visiting. I experimented with all kinds of scarves since most often I looked like a Russian *baba,* grandma, in a babushka—not very glamorous or attractive. Muslim women seemed to have the knack for looking gorgeous even when covered from head to toe in a black chador, the outer garment worn in Iran by observant Muslim women. Frustrated by how I looked in a head-cover, I blasphemed under my breath as I donned my scarf, "Allah is

Mahine, Jaleh's mother (left) and Carole out for tea in Esfahan, Iran (2005). By my second week in Iran I learned to wear a hijab that didn't make me look like a Russian grandmother. *The Carole J. Garrison Family Archive.*

great, Mohammed is his prophet and they both hate women, or at least they hate me." It was incorrect I admit, but saying it allowed me to vent my displeasure with forced clothing restrictions that included not only a head covering but long outer garments which added to my discomfort in the high heat of the Iranian summer.

There was one uncle, Hossein, a robust man in his mid to late sixties, who in keeping with Islamic law, would not shake my hand, and Allah forbid, no hugs. In everything else, he was gracious and friendly. One morning, my friend's father, Reza told me this uncle needed U.S. dollars for a hajj, which was occurring later that year

The last time he had exchanged money he had been cheated—given counterfeit bills.

"Would you mind to exchange some of your U.S. cash for Iranian money with Uncle Hossein?" asked Reza. Why not? I was still anticipating a few days shopping at the old bazaar and would need to exchange dollars anyway. Maybe the uncle would like me better. The two men took my cash and went off in a corner to figure out the exchange. I sat quietly unconcerned on the couch reading one of the few English language books in the house.

When they finished, Uncle handed me the Iranian rials. "Do you want to count the money?" asked Reza. "Uncle wouldn't want you to think you had been cheated."

I stared at them while thinking to myself, how in the hell could I know. I don't have clue what the exchange rate is or even how to read Iranian money." But to Uncle, I said, "No, I have no need to count it, I trust you completely." Reza translated.

I was squeezed in a massive bear hug, my breath coming in ragged heaves against his chest. Uncle held me so tightly I could hear his heart beat. The entry fee into this community was not money, not religion—it was trust.♦

CHAPTER 7
Roaches

I SIT STUDYING THE TINY chestnut-colored roach for a long moment, a mix of revulsion and irrational fear prickling across the back of my neck. When I see its antennae twitching, I realize it is studying me. We are joined in a contest to see who will move first. It stays frozen to the pale green wall, just above the white ceramic tile with its stained and yellowed grout. I tighten my hands into fists and will my foot not to tap on the floor.

I decide to concentrate on why I have such a strong emotional reaction to this tiny bug, not more than the size of a thumbnail. Unlike me, it is no threat. Packed inside my response to this tiny creature, however, is a dark abyss of fear and guilt.

Roaches have managed to sustain their species for more than 320 million years and have existed in human lore since classical antiquity. This little one, generally gregarious by nature, is probably desperate to escape and return to its multitudinous kin who, I'm certain, inhabit the warmer areas within the walls throughout the tenement building that I'm currently calling home. Like the varied immigrants who live here, roaches are popularly depicted as dirty pests and difficult to get rid of, though the great majority of the species—like the majority of immigrants—are inoffensive and live in a wide range of habitats around the world.

My roach doesn't move, save for an occasional spasm of its antennae. The bathroom light is on, and it's waiting for the cover of darkness to escape. Perhaps it doesn't want me to see the doorway to its route. In any case, my fear subsides and my thoughts turn to the connection of this creature to the financial and physical poverty of the home where I'm a guest.

My senses recreate the clash of smells in the halls at dinner time—pungent curries, savory soups, fresh bread and hot cooking oil—seeping through the thin doors of the more than fifty apartments on each floor of the eight-story building. I hear the loud scraping of furniture on the floor above being moved by its occupants from one corner to another as beds and tables are rearranged in preparation to sleep or eat in their tiny efficiency. I think of the tinfoil sheets Sonam and her neighbors hang to protect the kitchen walls from the grease of the cooking oil that's used to make almost everything the families in this building eat. Finally, I picture the gray streaked windows, muddied with smog from the heavily traveled city street below.

My attention returns to roaches, like this one, which are not just a synonym for poverty. They may be ubiquitous in old, run-down houses like those in this neighborhood, but they live lives parallel to the humanity that also inhabits these dwellings. Roaches have an intricate social structure involving shared shelter, social dependence, communication and kin recognition.

When Karma was born a few years ago, the family gave up the tiny room that had been used as a shrine to the Buddha and turned it into a second bedroom for the little boy. The three girls, now well out of their teens, still share the larger bedroom—leaving Sonam and her husband, Pasang, who work opposite shifts, to sleep on a couch amidst the clutter of the sitting room.

Carole and Sonam in Toronto, Canada turning the huge Tibetan prayer wheels at the local Buddhist community center, winter 2016. *The Carole J. Garrison Family Archive.*

The dining area is devoted to Karma's toys, bikes and strollers as well as kitchen supplies. When most everyone is home, the couch and settee are heaped with many arms and legs, each set of hands holding some sort of small electronic device. The flat screen TV shows only Netflix and YouTube, as no local channels are available.

An iPad, propped up against a book, is continuously connected to Sonam's elderly parents' home in Kathmandu so that anyone can chat as the urge strikes. Occasionally there is a squeal of laughter, some jostling so that an iPad or phone can be passed around and lots of elbowing before everyone gets comfortable again, using each other for warmth and connection.

Rice and a stack of flat bread are in bowls. Dishes and spoons, scrupulously washed a second time when taken from the cupboards, lay haphazardly on the bench that serves as a coffee table. The fragrance of sandalwood wafts through the apartment as incense smoke curls up from Buddha's shrine, which now occupies a quarter of the sitting area. Karma complains, "Smells like bug spray."

I am with them, and I am apart—half family member, half guest. I am mostly with them during family discussions and games or endlessly playing with Karma. I'm a guest when the next day's chores, schedules and responsibilities are assigned. When we go to celebrate the Dalai Lama's winning of the 1989 Nobel Peace Prize, still a cause de celebration twenty-seven years later, I wear clothes in colors most like a Tibetan monk's robes, orange and magenta, but my round eyes and light hair give me away.

Tomorrow I will leave them. Sonam already insists that they call Uber to take us to the Toronto airport, although I know the family will return home by trolley and a couple of busses. Still needing to be frugal with every penny in the communal pot, the children's lives, full of hardships, don't appear to be much different from the pretty girl with a quick smile and flashing eyes whom I met weaving rugs at the Tibetan refugee camp in Nepal. But they are. Gayki already has an RN degree and Tashi, the image of her mother as a young woman, is a semester away from graduating in hospitality management. Dechen, a typical college sophomore, still flounders between her passions and the practicalities of life.

The room seems brighter than when I first noticed my quiet companion. The roach has not moved, as if it's glued to the wall. I gather a paper towel into a ball, screwing up the courage to squish it. Its antennae twitch. A signal for help? For compassion? At that moment I think of Trump, president-elect of the United States, and his strident anti-immigrant comments. Those who buy his rhetoric would squish this family in the same way that I'm contemplating killing this bug. So I don't do it. ◆

CAMBODIAN JOURNAL: PART THREE

Preface

Cambodia's pull on me continued over the years, drawing me back and connecting me more deeply to the people. I took Tevi with me until she was in her teens, hoping to strengthen her self-identity. But actually, I went for me. I went because many of the people whose lives intersected with mine in the 1990s called me "Momma" with a reverence that I rarely experienced anywhere else. I went because, in Cambodia, I didn't just dream about being a warrior. I was one. ■

CHAPTER 1

Journal Entry: Kampongtrach Mountain
Kamput Cambodia, 2017

T HEY TAKE AWAY ALL THE BODIES. The smell too bad," the thin young Cambodian teenager tells me, his dark face solemn, his black eyes impenetrable. He is leaning up against an old motor bike covered in red dirt while I sit on a cement bench under a large, leafy tree on the edge of an open grotto. The bright blue sky is fringed in green leaves around the opening, about sixty feet up from the grotto floor. Roots and vines hang down, clinging to the rocky mountain wall. "Now I show you happy cave," the boy continues eagerly, gesturing with his flashlight for me to follow him.

I study the scar on his young face. I try to discern his emotions. After all, the Khmer Rouge threw thousands to their deaths in the 1980s from the top of this rocky mountain, leaving their bodies to rot in its many caverns. Maybe his grandparents died here, or maybe they were among the guerrillas who threw over their neighbors and kinsmen. I don't ask again if this is a "killing cave." Appearing to be relieved, he grins and tells me, "Come see. The cave has dragon head, and turtle. All by nature. No bats in daytime."

No bats. I like that. A young girl walks over—the boy's cousin. There is a small horde of kids, all competing for tourists to take through the caves. She sees me as a good mark and joins us. "Where are you from?" she asks in perfect English. None of the kids is a trained guide.

"The U.S. How many languages can you speak?"

She raises her eyes for a moment; then, with her right index finger, she points to each finger on her left hand—American, Barang, French, Germany, Italy, Australian—she names each finger. I don't correct her; I don't always understand Aussie speech myself. I like them, these ragamuffin kids. As I stand up to go with her and her cousin, I hear a commotion in the trees. Not bats, monkeys!

The girl takes my hand and leads me to a spot where I can get a better view. "Chit chit chit," she calls to a large caramel-colored monkey while a woman, who has just finished praying at the small shrine near the cave's entrance, throws candy up to it. Another monkey skitters down the vines and joins the first. Several backpackers gather around, eager to see something novel. The boy, whose name I now know is Pran, whispers conspiratorially in his choppy English, "These just little monkeys. The giant black one only comes down at night." A little tremor runs down my back.

Pran has shared a secret with me, so now I'm exclusively his client. We move into the cave. "Mind your head," his cousin calls after me. (An injured tourist does not give good tips.) Moving through the cave, we see rock formations carved out of the stone that date as far back as the Cambrian period of evolution. My tour lasts about ten minutes. The kids want me to follow them to another site, a cave pool. "You can swim, get cool. Cambodia hot," Pran coos.

Carole's young would-be guide at Kampong Trach Mountain, Kampot, Cambodia, 2017. These youngsters spoke several languages and told many tall tales about the mystical powers of the cave. *The Carole J. Garrison Family Archive.*

Nith, Carole, Nareth, with sons Norin and Purin, posing outside the cave entrance at Kampong Trach Mountain, 2017. *The Carole J. Garrison Family Archive.*

"Yes, *kadal nah,* very hot," I say, showing off my few Khmae words. I give them each four thousand riels, which equals about one U.S. dollar. They hang around a few minutes to see if I will change my mind but, when I don't move, the cousins go off in search of another prospect.

But I'm uneasy, unable to let go. I'm fixated on the Killing Fields. I'm still obsessing over the Vietnam War. I'm stuck in the 1990s, when Cambodia had a chance to leap from its thir- teenth century existence into the twenty-first with ease — as there was nothing to reconstruct, nothing to tear down. It could have reinvented itself. But Cambodia was unlucky. After supervising its first democratic election, the United Nations left it with a greedy, corrupt government. Now huge skyscrapers tower over squatters' shanties; there is no infrastructure or city planning. A thin veil of garbage covers the entire country, even here on this rural mountainside.

I want to discuss what happened here, the genocide that took place in and around these caves. But the children don't want to talk about what the Khmer Rouge did; that happened in the past, before they were born. Now Kampongtrach Mountain, Phnom Kampong Trach, provides them with an opportunity to make money. Maybe that is how it should be. I don't know.♦

CHAPTER 2

Journal Entry: A Cambodian Pinocchio
Phnom Penh, Cambodia 2017

I HAVE LOTS OF GRANDCHILDREN. Most are not related to me by blood, but by a bond of affection from my shared history with their parents. Several of them reside in Cambodia, the children of former staff who worked with me to end the country's long period of violence and civil war. Sometimes these grandchildren, like those related by kinship, go astray. Like Pinocchio, they fall in with bad company and face an uncertain future as they struggle to come of age.

We park in front of a high, cream-colored, corrugated sheet metal wall. It's only 9:00 a.m., but the sun is already high in the sky and the heat is shimmering off the dusty road. Nith grabs a few plastic bags of fresh food from the backseat as well as a small box of canned soda. I follow closely behind her. She rings the bell and a small flap in the sheet metal lifts, followed by the creak of the door swinging open for us to enter.

Several young men in black or khaki uniforms sit around the entrance, ask Nith a couple of questions and inspect our bags.

One of them escorts us to a cement picnic table with benches. There are a dozen or so similar tables in the large open area, where a few families sit together, talking with each other. At one table a young man holds a baby, his full attention drawn to its tiny face and hands. At another, a dark-skinned man with a hard face gulps down food from take-out containers while his visitors look silently on. We sit silently, watching.

"Can we see inside?" I ask Nith.

"No, not allowed," she replies. "We have thirty minutes only." More silence.

Nan, with a black-uniformed guard by his side, exits through a metal door into the visiting area. I can see a chain link fence behind the door. Although he's petit and young-looking for his age, almost fifteen, he appears to be healthy. I stand to greet him. Surprise crosses his face. "Grandma, hullo. I am happy to see you," he says eagerly in good English. Nan clasps me tightly around the shoulders; then he steps back, hands up as if in prayer, to greet me in the traditional Cambodian way. I remember that, years ago when I was in the country for a visit, he grudgingly went on family outings and hardly spoke to me. I hand him the bag of chocolates that I brought—M&Ms, Snickers and some local brands of candy.

The boy, his head closely shaven, moves to sit next to his mother, Nith. He strokes her arm, touches her, apologizes in whispers and asks when he can go home to see his little brothers. Another guard, this one dressed in a khaki-colored uniform, sits down with us. Not much older than the boy, he informs Nith that Nan has a rash on his body. She looks concerned and Nan pulls up his shirt to show her. It looks like dermatitis, possibly scabies.

I notice that Nan has two tattoos on his arms. One, which appears to be semi-professional script, says something about family; the other is his name written in crude block letters. He didn't have them eighteen months ago, the last time I was in Cambodia—before he was imprisoned.

Carole visiting Nan at the drug rehab center, Phnom Penh, 2017. I brought lots of chocolate, and we talked about football. *The Carole J. Garrison Family Archive.*

This guard, a recovering addict and Nan's mentor, speaks to him in Khmae, so his message is hard for me to follow. Nith explains that it's meant to be therapeutic. The guard is reminding Nan that he's not finished with his drug addiction treatment and that remaining in the rehab center is for his own good. The boy looks as if he's processing the message, but I can't tell if he's just on a charm offensive.

Nan had found a gang of boys on Facebook who said that he could join their soccer team. He didn't know that they were street kids and, in the beginning, they were more fun than school and studying. He didn't plan to get hooked on drugs, didn't plan to play hooky and didn't plan to lie. School was hard for him; the street kids offered him something more exciting to do. Now Nan has become like Pinocchio—wanting to repent, trying to be a real boy, hoping to make his father proud—but there is no blue-haired fairy who can save him.

Nareth, Nan's father, doesn't visit. He told me that "it's too hard on his heart." But Nan asks anyway: When will his daddy come to see him? Nith tells him that daddy is busy in Kampong Cham building a kitchen for his elderly parents. It's hard to tell if he believes her. I wonder if he knows that Nareth is afraid to bring Nan home for fear that he might corrupt his little brothers.

Our time is almost up. Nith gives the guard ten U.S. dollars to buy some medicated soap and other things for Nan. Everyone is getting anxious. Nan doesn't want us to leave; we don't want to go.

"Do you get to play football? What's your favorite team?" I ask, remembering that he loved football (soccer). He brightens and replies, "Yes, I play every day and study English." I smile approvingly. Nan resumes stroking Nith's arm until the guard in the black uniform comes to the table and signals for Nan to follow him back through the metal door, behind the chain link fence.

Nan's young mentor tells Nith to get a metal box for the food she brings to her son. The rats are eating his stuff.◆

CHAPTER 3

Journal Entry: Stolen
Phnom Penh, Cambodia 2017

S INCE WORKING IN CAMBODIA during the 1990s, I return often to visit old colleagues and close friends, and do the "tourista" thing—visit the royal palace, museums and the abundant souvenir shops. On any given day in present Phnom Penh, blinding sun beats down on the central courtyard of the 110-year-old National Museum of Cambodia. Tourists stroll along its lush tropical paths, take photos while blinking in the light and read the neatly printed information cards and boards. A gift shop volunteer hands out fragrant stalks of tiny white flowers in exchange for donations and smiles benevolently at foreign visitors' attempts to say Susaday—a shorthand, vaguely impolite version of "good morning" in Khmer.

The stone statues that make up the bulk of the collection have been recovered from art thieves and dealers, many of them returned grudgingly over the past twenty years by museums in the United States and Europe. There are fantastical sculptures of the monkey warrior Hanuman—the complicated, godlike figure who, with his monkey army, saved the beautiful princess Sita for the Hindu Prince Vishnu. Along with statues of Hanuman, are those of the bird-like Garuda, variations of the multi-armed Vishnu, and images the early Cambodian Buddhist king Jayavarman of the Angkor period which together fill the open-air passageways and colonnades with massive granite figures.

But it hasn't always been that way. When I first arrived in Cambodia in 1992 with the United Nations mission to implement the Paris Peace Accords to end the country's civil war and hold a national election, most locals had never seen these artifacts. Twenty-five years ago, the aged building was in a state of near collapse. Its collection had been destroyed, trafficked out of the country by the Khmer Rouge, scattered around the world, or slumbered in the jungle undergrowth protected from decades of civil war by randomly placed landmines. Not much changed in the several years I worked in Cambodia — but today's National Museum of Art is a national treasure that both locals and tourist enjoy. On my most recent trip, I marveled at the change in the museum but recalled an earlier time when Cambodians had a quite different response to Cambodia's rich trove of ancient art.

It was 1999, and I had a surprise visit to my home in Akron, Ohio from a Khmer friend, Weiling, who had managed to secure a visa to visit her ailing father in Los Angeles. "I know. Let's go up to the Cleveland Museum of Art, which has an exhibit of sculpture from the Angkor and other periods of Khmer history." As excited as she was to be visiting me in the States, my Cambodian friend would have said yes to any suggestion I made.

The art museum's large Indian and Southeast Asian gallery seemed to grow huge while Weiling, with fat tears rolling silently down her pink cheeks, appeared to shrink as she stood silently looking out over the thousand-armed bodhisattva, giant grey granite torsos of protective monkey demons, and the disembodied heads of Khmer kings who leered up menacingly like phantoms from disturbed ancient tombs. Even the peaceful

Weiling (left), Carole and Tevi (front) in Cleveland, OH circa 1998. Later we visited the Cleveland Art Museum only to find to Weiling's great distress, the galleries held more Khmer artifacts than she had seen in her life time of living in Cambodia. *The Carole J. Garrison Family Archive.*

Carole visiting with the Monkey gods at the National Museum of Art, Phnom Penh, Cambodia, 2017. The joy was seeing hundreds of returned artifacts and statues to the place where they belonged and once again accessible to Cambodians. *The Carole J. Garrison Family Archive.*

countenances of the many terracotta, granite and bronze Buddhas lining the walls appeared ill at ease.

The museum's brochure claimed that it owned a rich and expanding collection of ceramics from Vietnam, Cambodia, Thailand, Laos and Burma, as well as Hindu and Buddhist temple sculpture. However, the brochure did not include any images of the decapitated stone bodies, sometimes only their feet, which had been left behind to guard Cambodia's sacred and historical sites. It didn't explain that heads had been severed from toppled statues, to make them cheaper to ship, or that collectors had stolen them to grace coffee tables in upscale brownstones in New York City and Washington, D.C, before donating or selling them to museums when they changed their decor.

I joined Weiling, taking in the gallery's expanse, trying to see it through her eyes. Could I imagine the Statue of Liberty's arm perched on top of a family's credenza in a private residence? I conjured up a vision of headless statues of Washington and Jefferson on the D.C. mall; I even envisaged Chester's monument of Lincoln sitting in the chair with both of his famous hands missing, but the idea seemed preposterous. My lips didn't tremble as Weiling's did, although I recognized the anger that comes from being violated, the helplessness one feels in the aftermath of a theft. This exhibit represented the robbery of an entire culture, a rape of its most iconic possessions. She was devastated.

"Do you want to leave?" I whispered.

"I never saw such beauty in my homeland," she mumbled in response.

"Can't you appreciate seeing them, although the statues are here rather than in Cambodia?"

"Can you like to watch your mother stolen?"

We headed to the Monet gallery.

More than decade later the headline in the May 12, 2015, issue of The Plain Dealer read, "It's official: Cleveland Museum of Art returns Hanuman statue to Cambodia." I cut the article out, scanned it into my computer and emailed it to Weiling. It wouldn't make amends for the looting of Cambodia's art, but it was a small step towards healing the injustice and pain I had seen on Weiling's face that day at the Cleveland museum.

Now that Phnom Penh's National Museum is restored, many of Cambodia's stolen artifacts returned to its safe keeping. Each time a piece of looted Cambodia's history is found and retrieved is a time for celebration, but often, as with any violated victim, it opens old wounds that haven't healed — and never will. ♦

CHAPTER 4

Journal Entry: A Pilgrim's Journey
Phnom Penh, Cambodia 2017

HOPING THAT ONE OF HUN'S sisters would recognize me, I leaned my face out the car window as my driver, Kimsore, slowly drove down the crowded row of cell phone stores. No matter how many times over the years I had visited Hun's family, I could never recall the shop's address—only vaguely remembered the general location. Kimsore was prepared to go from store to store with Hun's story until someone could direct us to the right place. No need. I saw a face light up with recognition almost immediately. It belonged to a younger sister, nick-named Pheap, who bore a remarkable resemblance to Hun.

Before Kimsore came to a complete stop, I leapt from the car and ran to embrace Pheap. I leaned in over the counter, ignoring her bewildered customer, and kissed her face. Our hands fluttered as we tried to touch, connect, hug. Our greetings were a noisy, gushing mixture of Khmae and English.

Pheap came around from behind the counter, leaving her customer to unwillingly observe our reunion. As we stood, our hands clasped together tightly, I said the words I've repeated so many times, "I come so you know I never forget your sister."

At that moment, a great weight heaved against my chest, and my tears came quickly and violently. It has been nineteen years since Hun had begged me not to leave her, not to leave Cambodia—that I was her luck in Cambodia. It has been nineteen years since I received the phone call telling me that she had been murdered in a robbery. I have been coming back to Phnom Penh every few years since then—each time finding her family and seeking absolution, each time expecting it to be easier. It never is.

Pheap's eyes were sad but she smiled and said, "We never forget you. We know your heart."

The tears stopped like a spring rain passing quickly. I wiped a hand against my eyes, staining my fingers black. For some reason, seeing the wet mascara made me feel better. After a few more sniffs, I regained most of my composure. I asked Pheap about the rest of her family, about Hun's husband and daughter Mey-Mey who now lived in Paris, about herself. Her English was good enough to get the gist of my questions. Everyone was *karphakpiny*, fine. We joked about the time I had taken her and her sisters to the elegant Sofitel Hotel for dinner back in 1996, a happier time, a time before the political coup, before I left Cambodia for the safety of the US. They had spent half an hour in the ladies' room because they thought it was the most beautiful bathroom they had ever seen. As she joined me in remembering that special evening, Pheap's tinkling laughter was like a soothing balm.

Pheap invited me for dinner, but I declined. I had completed my mission. Kimsore and I left. I'm glad that my memory of Hun remains vibrant, that thinking about her death still brings me to tears. It makes me even happier to know that my continued pilgrimages to see her family lighten our hearts and soften the pain of loss.

Post Script:
From: Mey-Mey Kong
Sent: Wednesday, May 3, 2017 7:38 PM
To: Garrison, Carole
Subject: I search you for a long time.

Dear Carole,

I don't know if you can remember me but I remember you because you are my mom's friend. My mom is Cheeng Hun. I remember one time you came in Cambodia and you bought me a dress when I was 8. I am 21 years old know and I live in France. I hope we can keep contact and speak together.

Much love from Mey-Mey Kong.♦

Reunion with Hun's daughter Mey-Mey. Longjumeau France, August 29, 2017. *The Carole J. Garrison Family Archive.*

ABOUT THE AUTHOR

CAROLE J. GARRISON is a former police officer, professor, activist and passionate humanitarian. After a stint as a suburban house-wife and mother in Miami, she joined the Atlanta Bureau of Police Services in the early 1970s as one of a handful of women police officers but shifted to education after receiving her PhD from Ohio State University. During her career as an educator, she helped launch the University of Akron's Women's Studies pro-gram, was inducted into the Ohio Women's Hall of Fame, was vice president of Ohio's first women's commission, appointed by the U.S. president to the Department of Defense Committee on the Status of Women in the Military, and volunteered with the UN to help supervise Cambodia's first democratic election. In 1993, she returned to Akron to teach, but thee years later she returned to Cambodia and served as executive director of the Cooperation Committee for Cambodia, a network of humanitar-ian and developmental non-governmental organizations (NGO).

Her work has appeared in *VietNow Nation Magazine, The Sacrifice: What Would You Give? An Anthology of Inspirational Essays* (2014), *WHAT DOES IT MEAN TO BE WHITE IN AMERICA? Breaking the White Code of Silence, A Collection of Personal Narratives* (2016), and placed in the WOW! Women On Writing, Winter 2016 Flash Fiction contest, *The Wait.* Today, Garrison resides in Ona, West Virginia. Although retired as chair of the Department of Criminal Justice and Police Studies at Eastern Kentucky University, she continues to teach applied ethics and policing courses online. When not teaching or writing, she serves as an executive board member of the Friends of WV Public Broadcasting, Chair of the Board of Unlimited Future, a local Huntington business incubator, a docent at the Huntington Museum of Art, and is a member of the Huntington Women's Leadership Caucus. She is also a reader for fourth grade at Altizer Elementary School and a Girls on The Run volunteer at Nichols Elementary School. www.cjgarrison.com.◆

OTHER BOOKS BY 2LEAF PRESS

2LEAF PRESS challenges the status quo by publishing alternative fiction, non-fiction, poetry and bilingual works by activists, academics, poets and authors dedicated to diversity and social justice with scholarship that is accessible to the general public. 2LEAF PRESS produces high quality and beautifully produced hardcover, paperback and ebook formats through our series: *2LP Explorations in Diversity, 2LP University Books, 2LP Classics, 2LP Translations, Nuyorican World Series,* and *2LP Current Affairs, Culture & Politics.* Below is a selection of 2LEAF PRESS' published titles.

2LP EXPLORATIONS IN DIVERSITY
Substance of Fire: Gender and Race in the College Classroom
by Claire Millikin
Foreword by R. Joseph Rodríguez, Afterword by Richard Delgado
Contributed material by Riley Blanks, Blake Calhoun, Rox Trujillo

Black Lives Have Always Mattered
A Collection of Essays, Poems, and Personal Narratives
Edited by Abiodun Oyewole

The Beiging of America:
Personal Narratives about Being Mixed Race in the 21st Century
Edited by Cathy J. Schlund-Vials, Sean Frederick Forbes, Tara Betts
with an Afterword by Heidi Durrow

What Does it Mean to be White in America?
Breaking the White Code of Silence, A Collection of Personal Narratives
Edited by Gabrielle David and Sean Frederick Forbes
Introduction by Debby Irving and Afterword by Tara Betts

2LP UNIVERSITY BOOKS
Designs of Blackness, Mappings in the Literature and
Culture of African Americans
A. Robert Lee
20TH ANNIVERSARY EXPANDED EDITION

2LP CLASSICS
Adventures in Black and White
Edited and with a critical introduction by Tara Betts
by Philippa Duke Schuyler

Monsters: Mary Shelley's Frankenstein and Mathilda
by Mary Shelley, edited by Claire Millikin Raymond

2LP TRANSLATIONS
Birds on the Kiswar Tree
by Odi Gonzales, Translated by Lynn Levin
Bilingual: English/Spanish

Incessant Beauty, A Bilingual Anthology
by Ana Rossetti, Edited and Translated by Carmela Ferradáns
Bilingual: English/Spanish

NUYORICAN WORLD SERIES
Our Nuyorican Thing, The Birth of a Self-Made Identity
by Samuel Carrion Diaz, with an Introduction by Urayoán Noel
Bilingual: English/Spanish

Hey Yo! Yo Soy!, 40 Years of Nuyorican Street Poetry,
The Collected Works of Jesús Papoleto Meléndez
Bilingual: English/Spanish

LITERARY NONFICTION
No Vacancy; Homeless Women in Paradise
by Michael Reid

The Beauty of Being, A Collection of Fables, Short Stories & Essays
by Abiodun Oyewole

WHEREABOUTS: Stepping Out of Place,
An Outside in Literary & Travel Magazine Anthology
Edited by Brandi Dawn Henderson

PLAYS
Rivers of Women, The Play
by Shirley Bradley LeFlore, with photographs by Michael J. Bracey

AUTOBIOGRAPHIES/MEMOIRS/BIOGRAPHIES

Trailblazers, Black Women Who Helped Make America Great
American Firsts/American Icons
by Gabrielle David

Mother of Orphans
The True and Curious Story of Irish Alice, A Colored Man's Widow
by Dedria Humphries Barker

Strength of Soul
by Naomi Raquel Enright

Dream of the Water Children:
Memory and Mourning in the Black Pacific
by Fredrick D. Kakinami Cloyd
Foreword by Velina Hasu Houston, Introduction by Gerald Horne
Edited by Karen Chau

The Fourth Moment: Journeys from the Known to the Unknown, A Memoir
by Carole J. Garrison, Introduction by Sarah Willis

POETRY

PAPOLÍTICO, Poems of a Political Persuasion
by Jesús Papoleto Meléndez
with an Introduction by Joel Kovel and DeeDee Halleck

Critics of Mystery Marvel, Collected Poems
by Youssef Alaoui, with an Introduction by Laila Halaby

shrimp
by jason vasser-elong, with an Introduction by Michael Castro
The Revlon Slough, New and Selected Poems
by Ray DiZazzo, with an Introduction by Claire Millikin

Written Eye: Visuals/Verse
by A. Robert Lee

A Country Without Borders: Poems and Stories of Kashmir
by Lalita Pandit Hogan, with an Introduction by Frederick Luis Aldama

Branches of the Tree of Life
The Collected Poems of Abiodun Oyewole 1969-2013
by Abiodun Oyewole, edited by Gabrielle David
with an Introduction by Betty J. Dopson

2Leaf Press is an imprint owned and operated by the Intercultural Alliance of Artists & Scholars, Inc. (IAAS), a NY-based nonprofit organization that publishes and promotes multicultural literature.

NEW YORK
www.2leafpress.org